BROKEN ROAD

A Widower's Journey

BROKEN ROAD
A Widower's Journey

DARRIN DIXON

DLA Books

Great Falls, Montana

Published by DLA Books
88 Marmot Lane
Great Falls, MT 59404
ddixoncrna@hotmail.com

Names may have been changed to protect
the identities of the people involved.

Cover and interior design by Sara Glaser

Paperback ISBN: 9781974032303
eBook ASIN: B073W1M6CW

To Joan. Without you, I would not, could not have grown.

To Alex. Without you, I would not be alive today.

*To Loy. Without your unfailing love and support,
this book and the introspection from which it
was born would not have been possible.*

*To the amazing people from Choices Seminars who
helped me remember my dream of writing.*

*To Liz who believed in me, and pulled this story out of me
piece by piece, and in the process became a dear friend.*

To Monica who helped me hone this into what it is.

To Katrina and Sara for the finishing touches.

I know that nothing good lives in me, that is, in my sinful nature. For I have the desire to do what is good, but I cannot carry it out. For what I do is not the good I want to do; the evil I do not want to do—this I keep on doing. Now if I do what I do not want to do, it is no longer I who do it, but it is sin living in me that does it.

ROMANS 7:18–28

But he said to me, "My grace is sufficient for you, for my power is made perfect in weakness." Therefore, I will boast all the more gladly about my weaknesses, so that Christ's power may rest on me. That is why, for Christ's sake, I delight in weaknesses, in insults, in hardships, in persecutions, in difficulties. For when I am weak, then I am strong.

2 CORINTHIANS 12:9–10

Contents

PART I

Player and the Girl Next Door

The first time I happened into Dr. Joan Anderson in the back corridor of Wilford Hall U.S. Air Force Medical Center, I strode confidently, importantly, daring bystanders to look at me, as I moved through the mass of stretchers and equipment strewn around me. She walked as though she were invisible, head slightly bowed, eyes directly to the front and lowered enough to not make eye contact. I was a recently-graduated, award-winning nurse anesthetist—number two in my class of forty in my top-five rated school, number one in my class of fellow anesthesia residents. Given my choice of any assignment in the Air Force, I'd been personally asked by my commander to remain at Wilford Hall, the Air Force's largest teaching hospital. Mecca. I was already a respected clinical instructor, a member of an elite mobile surgical team, and a part-time member of several joint medical groups working at the very tip of the military medicine spear. She was a first year anesthesiology resident—barely above an intern which was barely above a medical student which was barely above whale shit as I had learned on my first day of anesthesia school. In a clinical specialty that rewarded smoothness, I was butter, she was raw milk, still unchurned by experience.

Yet, as she moved toward me, something about her drew me in. Though she was attempting to remain unnoticed, I was enthralled. Her posture was impeccable. Her proportions, even under her ubiquitous green scrubs, were doll-like, a caricature, ever so slightly unrealistic in their perfection. Her skin was a flawless olive color; her face a welcoming ovoid shape, lips full and defined with a slight pout, but also a perpetual upturn at the outer edge which hinted but didn't fully commit to a smile. These attributes all paled in comparison to her eyes though—alive, unnaturally large, the rich color of molten milk chocolate with shimmering butterscotch highlights. She was very much the "girl next door," but with a twist that I couldn't for a moment grasp. Then it came to me—with a certainty I'd never known. She was the one I was supposed to marry.

We exchanged names after I surreptitiously glanced at the nametag positioned just above the swell of her left breast. God, I hoped she didn't think I was ogling what was obviously something very special.

"Pleased to meet you, Dr. Anderson."

She replied with a soft and happy, "Just Joan, please. Doctor seems a little pretentious, don't you think? Besides, we've met before."

"As you wish, 'Just Joan,' especially since we're old friends. Welcome to my department."

I couldn't recall where we'd met or even that we had. Slightly disoriented and thrown off my usual flawless game, I did the only thing I could think of. Quickly making a lame excuse, I fled, attempting to make sense of why I'd failed to come up with my usual suave or endearing comment. My heart raced and my palms were moist. She was the girl of my Midwest childhood—could easily have fit into a Norman Rockwell painting—definitely not the type of woman I'd been attracted to up to this point in my life.

I escaped to the office I shared with one of my best friends—and perfect foil—Kathy. Right on the intersection of the busiest hallway in the vast hospital the two of us "owned," our office was a gathering spot for the bored, the busy, and the curious. As I entered, Kath lounged as usual at her desk, feet up, gourmet roast coffee in hand while her student was busy monitoring a patient in the operating room. In the short year we'd known each other, she had become my sounding board, co-conspirator, and best friend, a duty she shared with my other best friend, Mike. I already relied heavily on her instincts, especially about my rather busy "personal"-but-not-exactly-"love" life. I had never been in love.

Kathy and I could have been twins except for the fact that I was a tall, blond, Dutch/German man from the country. She was a short, dark-haired, Polish woman from the city. She'd come into the department like a tornado, marching with a purpose, head held high, chin leading the way, short legs churning. She made no bones about the fact that she was the boss. Boss of her students, boss of her colleagues, boss of the anesthesiologists, even boss of whatever surgeon and resident she happened to be working with. They all responded the same way—acquiescence. There was just something about her that garnered respect. From everyone. I'd seen her as a usurper to my throne initially, but the way she carried herself, her outspoken disdain for those in the department who were not quite up to her standards, and her blatant disregard for all of the many Air Force rules and regulations quickly won me over. I knew I'd found a sister and co-conspirator the day our boss, Colonel Kelly, walked into the office in an uncharacteristic huff to ask if Kathy had accepted San Antonio Spurs tickets as a gift (i.e., bribe) from a pharmaceutical rep. With an innocent look on her face she said, "Yes."

Colonel Kelly replied, "Umm, you know that is against the Uniformed Code of Military Justice and you could be kicked out of the Air Force, don't you?"

Kathy's only retort: "Oh."

The Colonel, clearly at a loss, said, "Well, at least she's honest!" as he shook his head, turned around, and left the office. The matter was never brought up again. I'd never gone so far as to accept Spurs tickets. I'd just slept with a female rep or two.

Kathy was the best CRNA I had ever known, still is. We were similarly gifted with our hands and intellect. We were also ambitious and able to accomplish virtually any given task (if one didn't really care whether it was done by the rules). We were subsequently shown a high level of respect from surgeons down the line. Regularly requested to provide anesthesia for our commander, a major general (two star) (trauma surgeon). We were given the most challenging surgical cases. We were also given the brightest and highest functioning residents to mentor. As an added bonus, we were admitted into the physician anesthetist's inner sanctum as near equals to drink coffee and bullshit while our various residents babysat our cases. I was not surprised to find Kathy sitting at her desk.

In a rushed sentence I blurted out, "Kathy, I just met the most interesting and beautiful woman ever!"

Kathy said, "Slow down, Big Fella. Is her name Kris?"

"No, her name is not Kris. I've given up all Krisses for Lent. From now on Joan—only Joan."

"You're not even Catholic, Dumbass."

"Nope, not Catholic, but this is love at first sight—absolutely."

The year before, while breaking up with Deb, the trauma surgery resident I'd been dating for nearly five years, I'd begun dating several other women, each named a variation of Kris—which was also creepily my mother's name. There was Kris with a "K" whom I'd met while sitting on the patio of Carrabba's Italian Grill with Kathy and her husband Elmer prior to a night on the town. She was sexy and funny and young. She was also mysterious. One morning I'd found myself in her bed, with absolutely no recollection of what had happened after a night of sushi and only one beer. I remember beginning to kiss her, then nothing. I think she may have drugged me. I also thought she might be a spy. There was Christy "hair cut girl" who worked at the swanky salon where I had my very short hair trimmed every two weeks. She was cute as hell and very energetic. Then there was just plain Kristy who was a nurse. She was older and rather ordinary, but comfortable and undemanding—something I highly valued at the time. Also, she was my easiest revenge on Deb whom I believed had cheated on me while at a surgery conference in Hawaii. Kristy and Deb sometimes worked side by side in the medical ICU. Each woman served a purpose, but none inspired me.

Now I said, "I'm in love Kath, really. She's different."

"You're not in love, Stupid. Ever horny, but never in love. You're destined to be a man-whore your whole life. I'm kind of jealous actually." She said it with a little wink, but I knew she was only kind of kidding. I had always sensed that she'd also been created to remain free. She seemed to understand my longings, and I marveled at how she and her husband, Elmer, seemed to make their marriage work despite her own obvious appetites. Though I sensed in her a kindred

restless spirit, she never expressed anything but deep love and affec-
tion for her stalwart husband. And I was beginning to see why. He
was her grounding pad. The person who kept her from careening
out of earth's orbit.

"Well, I'm always slightly horny as a baseline," I said, "but I'm
not kidding. She's the most beautiful woman I've ever met! Even my
mother would approve."

My mother had not loved Deb.

Kathy was quiet then. She knew my habit of convincing women
to date me and then losing interest. She had only recently sent me
on a blind date several thousand miles away to meet a good friend of
hers who was stationed in California. Her friend and I'd had a good
time. In fact, we'd had a fabulous time, mostly in her bedroom, on
her kitchen counter, and in the shower, but I did not fall in love with
her. She didn't fall in love with me, either. We both knew the day I
arrived that we were not destined to be together forever, but that fact
didn't keep us from enjoying one another and our weekend together.
She'd shown no hard feelings by sending me a hilarious gift as a me-
mento following our weekend tryst—an amazing life-like toy tongue
which expanded when exposed to water. Kathy laughed as she gave
it to me and watched as we let it soak and grow in a clear surgical
suction canister on our office desk.

Kathy interrupted my daydream by asking, "When are you leaving for Honduras?"

I glanced at the calendar behind her. "Week and a half."

Kathy's eyebrows arched in the particular way they did when she
was questioning me. "Did you tell her?"

"No, I only just met her!"

"You'd better tell her."

"Will you do some recon for me?"

"God, you're weak."

"Thorough," I said with my best roguish smile.

Honduras was a pertinent issue. In less than two weeks, I would fly to the middle of an overgrown jungle to spend a lovely month or so with my surgical team performing eye, ear, nose, and throat surgery on locals who didn't normally have access to the kind of care we were able to provide—a humanitarian/training mission for us. On this type of "soft" mission, we were able to practice surgery in austere environments to tune up for our next deployments which might not be "soft." A great opportunity for the local people, a priceless one for us. We would hold clinic and operate on between two and three hundred people in those few weeks.

I had only just returned from Denver, Colorado as part of a security team for the Big Eight Summit. I was busy. I was mysterious and random. I was on my way to accomplishing my goal of being a spook, and I relished this role. My frequent unexpected departures and habitual on-call status added to my mystique. I imagined the women I dated loved it, too.

Honduras was overshadowed by a choice I would have to make. I'd been invited to be part of an elite Special Operations medical team. Not merely a team of everyday medics, but a team of highly skilled medical personnel/warriors regularly deployed with no advance notice to places many hadn't heard of for occasions that didn't often make the national news. I would be required to be gone for more than ten months a year. I was also subtly urged to remain single. Thrilled to be asked, I was exhilarated to serve my country in a way that many couldn't—intoxicated by the travel, and status, and real live danger. I was most enamored by the prospect of finally becoming a tier-one elite warrior and integral part of our warfighting machine.

Military service wasn't something I'd been pushed to do as a child. Other than a few relatives drafted during wartime and a great uncle who'd been a U.S. Army Air Corp pilot, there were no military members in my family. As a child, though, I had wanted to be a soldier just like all the other boys my age. I would have recurring visions—not dreams, they always happened during the day—of me in the place of my G.I. Joe doll and his all-terrain vehicle with missiles, radar, computers, and a whole stock of weapons. My parents hadn't bought these toys; they were hand-me-downs from an older neighbor boy. Dad didn't exactly love me playing with a doll, even a G.I. Joe, and Mom wouldn't have imagined this would lead me into the military. In their minds, I was destined to be a nine-to-fiver with a conservative but lucrative job and a lovely nuclear family.

And yet, my parents had in their own way fostered my love for the military. I learned to shoot at an early age hunting and target practicing with my dad, and our home was structured in a very military way, with a very definite chain of command and duties assigned to each of us. I also have vivid memories of marching with two neighbor boys in our local "Old Settlers" parade in 1976, resplendent in our civil war uniforms—me with a bandage over my fake head wound as I banged on my drum in our own little fife and drum corps, watching the people stand as we marched by with the American flag flying proudly, celebrating our bicentennial. I couldn't suppress my sheer joy at my role and the crowd's response.

Along with my dreams of military glory, I wanted to become a man worthy of my parents' respect. Service was crucial to that. Though military service was really never discussed, service to others was. I believed that I could combine both service to my country and service to others—a win/win as far as I was concerned. The two weren't at all synonymous to my parents. When I broke the news that I was joining the Air Force, they were a little less than thrilled. Their idea of service to others was for me to sponsor a darling little African child, or help build a local church, even go on the occasional mission trip. It's not that my parents didn't want me to serve my country, they were just being protective and passing on what they'd learned. In their world, service was not something that would require me to move thousands of miles away, and it was certainly not something that would end with me on the wrong side of a weapon or in the arms of a foreign woman.

Back in Iowa where I'd grown up, family was considered even more important than service to anyone else. Service to family was the pinnacle of growth, maturity, and Christian values in our home. Though I may have been applauded by some for joining the military as a young man, I was always expected, after one short stint, to return to my small town and make my permanent home near my sisters, cousins, aunts, uncles, and grandparents, not be outside the fold gallivanting around the world being shot at and sowing my wild oats. The woman I would choose to be my wife would be required to meet a tightly defined set of characteristics. She'd have to be attractive enough to carry on and add to our gene pool (definitely Caucasian—we were from the heart of the lily-white Midwest), a hard worker, intelligent, required to absolutely adore children, and yearn to have at least three offspring. Lastly, and above all, she would have to be a Christian. At that time in my life, "Christian" was nothing more than a nebulous term describing someone who attended church on a regular basis, sang in the choir, and was a "good" person who encompassed all of the afore mentioned attributes—at least on Sundays. The rest of the week, our actions were up to interpretation.

This definition was only loosely paired with being a follower of Jesus Christ. Meeting Joan had created a conflict. Before Joan, I hadn't given marriage a second thought. Finding "the one" had seemed impossible. Or maybe I just wasn't ready to be monogamous. After meeting her, I was befuddled. Here was the only woman who could meet my family's high standards, a woman with whom I could settle down. But settling down conflicted with my military goals. Which did I really desire? The two seemed mutually exclusive.

I ran into Kathy in the hallway the next day, and with a slight knowing grin, she reported that she had already struck up a friendly relationship with Joan. Kathy was, well, tenacious. She was also utterly loyal to those she loved. She loved me. And because she loved me she did me these favors. We decided to meet for dinner to discuss Joan further.

That evening I met up with Kathy and Elmer at a local Italian restaurant á la "The Godfather" complete with fat, dark, olive-skinned men with greasy hair, hooded eyelids, and large white toothy smiles—a sure sign they were mafia. At least that's what my imagination allowed me to see. Each time I dined there, I was transported back—me slumped on my parents' bright orange couch as a teenager, watching "The Godfather" trilogy over and over, fully immersed in a cinematic gangster culture, a culture which had always seemed second only to a military career and eventual life as a secret agent where excitement abounded and women flocked, and glory was mine and mine alone—never to be shared, only alluded to, because it was so highly classified. Whatever the atmosphere, the food and wine were fantastic and the dessert sublime.

Before we even ordered Kathy began. "She's way too sweet for you."

Elmer settled back in his chair to observe the show. He narrowed his eyes ever so slightly, and a faint knowing smile appeared on his face, arms folded as always when the wheels of his mind were spinning—the antithesis of his flamboyant wife.

"Well, let's get right to it then. Thanks for your vote of confidence, Kath!"

"Besides, you've already met her. She was Deb's medical student the month you two broke up."

She added this last little morsel with a wry smile of her own.

"Oh shit. That's where we met!"

I thought of those months after Deb. Before Deb, I'd been a one-woman man, but after her, I'd begun pursuing "targets of opportunity"—first Kris, then Christie, then Kristy, choosing to be whomever I wanted to be with each of the women I was with. Keeping them separate had been the only critical issue. I'd been over a thousand miles from my family and light years distant from God, with no one to judge or wag their finger at my "sin." Supported, even urged on by my friends, I'd been reborn a player.

And Joan had been witness.

[2]

What Goes on TDY Stays on TDY

I left Texas for Honduras the third week in June. Before leaving, I learned from my personal spy that Joan's birthday was June 24th. I was good at occasions. A surprise birthday card ostensibly sent from somewhere "down range" would be a perfect opportunity to play my most cherished role. I asked Kathy to do another little favor and place that special birthday card—which I was happy to spend an inordinate amount of time picking out—in the mail to Joan while I was away. The card would be small and lighthearted. I didn't yet know what kind of sense of humor Joan possessed so I kept it cute, funny, and modest to keep from frightening her. A small card with kittens and balloons and an amusing line or two about her birthday. Nothing audacious, nothing at all controversial or risqué. She seemed innocent. I certainly didn't want to come across as desperate or overbearing or shallow or too serious or worst of all, nasty. Truth be told though, with that one little card, I was already out of my depth with Joan. Though she might not yet have been smooth at anesthesia, she was clearly head and shoulders above my current choices in women in intelligence and poise. I was so completely drawn to her that my practiced swagger seemed empty and phony even to me. All of a sudden, I desperately wished to be her white knight riding in on my white stallion to carry her to our castle in the perfect forever-after— something I had never desired to be for anyone. I was more comfortable as the strong, quiet, mysterious type. I was sure that a personal birthday greeting sent while south of the border, serving my country, on a humanitarian mission, would help her see our personal fairy tale my way and position me solidly in the wooing department.

The surprisingly short plane ride to Honduras was the last time I thought of Joan, my newfound compulsion, for the five weeks I remained in-country. Each time I boarded a plane for a mission, any mission, my mind threw a subconscious switch—turning off my life in the States and on to the mission at hand. The journey was the exhilarating upswing—a time to think only about what was to come in the near future. Never knowing what to expect, my heart rate always skyrocketed as we coasted in for a landing. Sometimes headed into harm's way, sometimes not. What I did know was that when we arrived at our destination, after our initial burst of adrenaline and frenetic activity preparing our gear, we would more than likely find ourselves with surprisingly little to do. Until the shit hit the fan. I always kind of hoped the shit would hit the fan. We all did. That's why we chose to do what we did. This particular mission was "soft," however. We would not be exposed to danger, other than flying into the second most dangerous airport on the planet, then traveling by road in caravan to San Pedro Sula, a city currently off limits to American military personnel (except us, the elite) because it was considered one of the most violent cities in the world.

We flew impossibly low over the mountain range, immediately diving into a long valley, a large city in view at the extreme limit of our vision. One moment we were skimming the mountain tops just above the clouds, the next streaking much too fast and dangerously low over the largest shanty town I had ever seen. I recalled reading just a few months before that a U.S. Air Force cargo plane—identical to the one we were currently in—had crashed off the end of the runway at this very airport, killing three active duty airmen. I sat straighter in my seat and grasped my armrests just a little tighter. In with a cleansing breath to maintain calm, I felt "ground effect" arrest our descent, and we glided on a cushion of air to the middle of the runway. Finally, with the loud chirp of tires on asphalt and a jolt as we strained against our seatbelts, the reverse thrust of the engines brought us to an abrupt halt.

Our team did not seem to be subject to customs, adding to my overall sense of being one of the "chosen." So after deplaning, we moved rapidly toward three white vans awaiting our arrival. We were always picked up in white vans. They were the Central American version of our black U.S. government SUV. Each van came complete with a Honduran national driver. I was pretty sure they were spies—like in Robert Ludlum's books about Jason Bourne.

I'd always wanted to be like Jason Bourne, an understated hero, an enigma—someone who saved the world, but merely shrugged it off as another day at the office, someone who cared less about fame and glory than the simple fact that he was making a difference or that he was really changing the world. Jason was an enigma, just like I desperately wanted to be. I was willing to do most anything to become like him. Nothing to do with accolades. Nothing to do with power or money. I wanted to feel confident, feel selfless, feel like my dad would be proud of me for doing important things, but allowing others the credit. Of course the nonstop action was always a draw too...

The road to San Pedro Sula was long. The highway was sometimes two lanes, sometimes less. Myriad trucks, small automobiles, motorcycles, scooters, and bicycles—not to mention the scruffy skinny dogs and occasional pig and scrawny chicken—did not appear to adhere to any type of traffic law. The road was tree-lined and lush in some places and completely bare, desert-like, and slightly ominous in others. We passed shack after shack, and small roadside stands—little but bare earth, dust, and scraps of wood and metal. Each new mission required me to transition immediately from my air-conditioned home and office to true third world surroundings. This mission was no different. We arrived in San Pedro Sula, zig-zagging in a manner directly out of the counter intelligence textbook for evasive driving, through successive barrios. Oddly each had a bank. There seemed to be an unusually large number of banks. Each bank was replete with a manned machine gun nest on the top, apropos in the bank robbery capital of the world.

We escaped chaos as our vans entered the tranquility of the luxury resort we would call home for the next five weeks, through a large white concrete fence with a wrought iron gate manned by armed security guards. The weather was sultry, oppressive, the sky a dirty brownish gray, and the air completely, eerily still. The humidity was 90%, and after stepping out from the air-conditioned van, my clothes immediately became damp, clinging to my skin. But we walked through large, hand-carved wooden doors to a completely different world. The floors were polished marble, the air crisp and cold. Everyone was well dressed, even the lowliest wait staff in their navy blue uniforms. We were shielded from the poverty and chaos surrounding our castle walls.

I spied her almost as soon as I walked through the door. Behind the front desk chatting with a guest, aloof and cool, but pleasant in her purpose. Her skin was the color of *café con leche*, hair dark brown and shoulder length. She was small in stature, but very well proportioned—slightly wider hips of the Latin American women, fuller lips. Her dark skin and eyes contrasted beautifully with her fashionable off-white linen pant suit that was as fresh as if it had just been laundered. I ambled confidently toward her place at the desk and quietly awaited my turn though other attendants were available. I was daydreaming about how she would look undressed. Would her caramel colored skin be uniform over her entire body, or would she have a bikini line? Would her nipples be the color of coffee? Would she have a slight rise in her stomach just above her pubic hair? Would she have body hair at all?

"Hello beautiful," I said in Spanish, "my name is Darrin. I am part of a group from the United States military here on a humanitarian mission. We're here to check in." Hardly an adequate come-on to a woman as beautiful as she who spoke Spanish, the most beautiful language I'd ever heard or learned. Nonetheless, whether my awkwardness amused her or because she saw something she liked, her sumptuous lips turned up slightly as she caught the word "beautiful."

Her dark eyes flashed as she said, "I would be happy to check you in, Sir, and thank you for coming to my country to help our people. You are very kind."

I was too full of myself to think she might be being sarcastic.

My reply was a simple, "Thank you." With my very best gleaming white smile.

She asked, "Is there anything else I can do for you?"

I grinned. "We'll see."

Our surgical team worked sixteen hour days, first screening hundreds of prospective patients, then performing surgery after surgery with equipment that was easily fifty years out of date. Most of my colleagues back home in their ivory tower teaching institutions wouldn't have had the slightest idea how to use those archaic anesthesia machines. Our "hospital" contained no air conditioner; one of our operating rooms had only a small window in one end with no glass and no ability to keep the bugs or birds out. We operated in shorts and tank tops, always soaked in sweat. After such grueling days, I didn't think of Joan. I did, however, find time for other things—starting with that first evening when the *café con leche* receptionist knocked on my door, ready for a drink on the rooftop patio and a tour of her luxury hotel.

Although many of the team members went straight to their rooms after returning to our hotel each evening, my routine was to catch a quick workout in the hotel gym, swim in the tepid pool, then go for a five-dollar massage performed by a beautiful Honduran woman who, if I tipped well up front, would make it "full body." After a quick shower, I usually retired to the rooftop bar for a drink with my new Honduran friend/front desk person/lover and finished off the public part of my night with a fat, hand-rolled Honduran cigar, sometimes dipped in cognac. In the confines of my hotel room with the sultry fading light filtering through the water-laden air, the color of her complexion, her passion in bed, the smoothness of her skin, and the slight huskiness of her voice as she became aroused all kept me up late. The way she sought not only to please me in multiple ways, but also frantically to bring herself to orgasm, was mind-altering. I fell completely under her spell.

Towards the end of our time in Honduras, I also met a group of young Dutch school teachers. I surprised them by being able to speak and understand their conversations. My hometown was near a small Dutch community in central Iowa where the town's old-timers were only too happy to teach me their mother tongue. I smiled inwardly as I realized many of those good "God fearing" folks would have been quite distressed to imagine how I used their beloved language. These young women were completely different than my new Honduran friend—tall, blonde, fair, much more angular than the Latin American women I had become acquainted with, also much quieter. Just the same, they intrigued me. Their language and accent was alluring, but mostly they were so much more, shall we say, open minded about things and willing to experiment. Considering myself a scientist (one who studied women), I did not resist.

Everywhere we went, we were treated as rock stars. Dining with governors and local officials, we were chauffeured around the cities in our extended white van/limos. Many times, we were offered our choice of escorts, and we were surrounded by hordes of curious local citizens because of our obvious difference in genetics—especially in the poor sections outside the city. I had dreamed of immersing myself in another culture as a spy ever since reading my first espionage novel. In my dreams though, I was able to blend in. Here I was tall, blond, and hairy, very noticeably different from the shorter, more slightly built, dark haired, dark skinned locals. Eventually I became "El Rubio," the blond one, or "Picaro," the crafty one. Not exactly the way I wanted to blend in as a spy, but being noticeable had its perks. Women noticed me. They also seemed to like to touch me.

Early in my career, I'd been let in on an old military axiom: "What goes on TDY (temporary duty) stays on TDY," and I certainly took that saying to heart. When I "sent" Joan a birthday card from

Honduras while being entertained by other women, I actually failed to see anything strange or even contradictory about the act. Having someone to ground me at home, even though I was being urged to remain single, seemed like a good thing. I was fully committed, in my own admittedly juvenile way, to making our relationship as good for Joan as it was for me—if in fact our relationship ever began, which I never for a moment doubted. Conversely, encouraged to do so by my mentors, the women I met and used in various parts of the world were to be considered casual stress-relief, comfort in my uncertain, highly-fluid world.

After a little over a month in Honduras, land of five dollar massages and cheap entertainment, where my only responsibility was to be in the operating room able to perform anesthesia by seven in the morning, I returned to the real world of San Antonio where I would be teaching clinical anesthesia each day, following the much stricter rules of the regular U.S. Air Force and again wooing the woman I believed could be the ONE.

3

The Marryin' Kind

Kathy and Elmer picked me up from the airport as the late afternoon sun sent shimmers across the tarmac.

Kathy, leaning forward in her seat, hardly able to contain herself, began immediately. "You wouldn't believe the case I did the other day!"

"Not as wild as the cases we did in Honduras. And, oh yeah, there were a few women."

"Shocking. But me first!"

I laughed. "You're always first! Elmer, is it like this in bed with her?"

He probably blushed. I don't remember, but I enjoyed attempting to get a reaction from him.

Kathy and I were like twins. Elmer, the wiser more mature sibling/father. Kath and I were type "A," very motivated, highly social, and highly self-absorbed. Elmer, a Zen master.

He pulled out of the airport parking lot.

"Kath, did you give Joan her card?"

"Of course. Would I let you down?"

"Haven't yet..."

"She said it was a nice gesture."

"What does that mean?"

"It means she thinks it was a nice gesture."

"What am I supposed to do with that?"

"Let's talk about it while we get you and Elmer some entertainment."

The three of us headed to a somewhat upscale (at least by strip joint standards) establishment named Champions, ironically the place I met the last girl that had even come close to being a keeper in my life. She was a nice young girl from Nebraska studying paleontology in college, and she was working her way through school as a waitress in this strip club. I hadn't been sure how that would play with my parents, but in the end it didn't matter. We'd had fun—platonic fun, at least in the Bill Clinton version of platonic—but eventually, our relationship dissolved as we both moved on. Kath, Elmer, and I casually entered, watching the strippers slide around various poles. Kathy amused, Elmer interested, and I slightly confused about Kathy's willingness to bring her husband here.

My training in marital relations began and ended with my parents, who for years co-existed but were not especially warm. They lived in the same home, parented the same children—albeit in shifts because both of them worked. They were both completely committed to the three of us in their own way, but mostly separately, unless they were attending a sporting, theatrical, or other school event. They traveled together on family vacations, but I never got the sense that they were in love. At least the head-over-heels-I-can't-live-without-you sort of love, the love I believed I would someday find. They held their children—and therefore their family—in a very committed, but mostly businesslike arrangement that wouldn't necessarily endure without us. I noticed early on that they never went out to have fun without us. Once as a teenager, after my aunt and uncle announced they were divorcing, I asked my mother if she and dad would divorce, too. It seemed they hadn't talked in months, not even to fight. But then again, I never saw them even disagree. Ever. My mom shrugged her shoulders and said, "I don't think so." They attended church together and community functions, certainly not strip clubs.

I tore my eyes away from the nubile young woman slowly winding herself down the pole in the center of her runway lighted stage and caught Elmer whispering playfully in Kathy's ear. She smiled in a way that was only meant for him, though if I hadn't known them, I wouldn't have picked up the emotion in it. Even at a strip club, there was only one woman for Elmer and one man for Kathy. After Elmer finally excused himself to visit the men's room, I asked, "How do you do this?" and gestured at the stage where another young woman began dancing with a live python.

Her reply was simple, "Elmer doesn't come to a club like this unless I ask him. When I take him, he gets to see, but not touch, a bunch of naked women and get all charged up with me as a chaperone. We get to go home together and let off a little pent up steam. Win-win." I wondered how Joan would feel about taking me to watch naked young women dance and guessed it probably wasn't going to happen.

———

Later that weekend, I met Kathy and Elmer again, this time out-side Colonel Kelly's house, the venue for our anesthesia department's "Hail and Farewell Soiree." Kathy had told me Joan would be there because the party was mandatory for residents. Colonel Kelly was our boss, my mentor, and what Navy people would call my "Sea Daddy." He was a mischievous character with thinning snow white hair and a tiny Errol Flynn mustache, also white. His hair gave the impression that he was fairly old. And he may have been, considering he was the highest ranking nurse anesthetist in the Air Force—a full "bird" Colonel. His next promotion would have been to brigadier general—a rank he would never attain by his own admission. Deeply tanned at all times of the year, his face was weathered and lined with what could have been age, but just as easily life experience. No one really knew for sure. He never said. I think his reticence was part of his cultivated mysterious facade. No matter his age, he acted perpetually young and was proudly contrary to the generals who outranked him. Like a leading man from the old western movies of my youth—wise, calm, a little rough around the edges, but always gallant, and always flirtatious with his leading woman—he had a persona I was actively trying to adopt.

We'd met two years prior when I was an anesthesia resident. One Friday afternoon, Colonel Kelly approached me and asked, "Lieu-tenant Dixon, are you on call this weekend?"

"Yes, Sir."

"Have you seen my new office?"

"No, Sir."

"Well, let me take you there."

"Yes, Sir."

He walked with a swagger. I didn't yet know him. I'd only heard the rumors. He had just arrived at Wilford Hall, but his reputation preceded him. After a short walk—me behind and to his left—we arrived at his office in the back corner of the same hallway in which I'd run into Joan. The office was sparsely furnished with utilitarian brown metal furniture. The only picture on the otherwise bare wall was a picture of a much younger Captain Kelly with several of his buddies—lily white asses mooning the camera, each man's butt cheek tattooed with a pair of green feet—the Jolly Green Giant—mark of a pararescue jumper.

"Do you like this furniture, Lieutenant?"

"Umm, no, Sir."

"Do you think it's befitting a full bird colonel?"

"No, Sir."

"I would love some new furniture, Lieutenant Dixon."

"Yes, Sir."

That was the end of the conversation.

Monday morning, the Colonel arrived to find brand new, higher end (the best I could abscond with from another office in the hospital), government issue office furniture. He never asked where it came from, but after that weekend I began to get opportunities to do things—opportunities I hadn't known existed.

The Colonel's house was perched in the hills on the far west side of San Antonio. From the front his home was lovely, but not ostentatious. We walked onto a nicely manicured yard with a small concrete slab as an entrance landing. The house was white with black accents, but the door was colored bright red—fitting Colonel Kelly's personality to a "T"—all buttoned up and proper on the outside with just a hint of the rebel within.

The Colonel himself answered the door with a drink in his hand.

Every time I saw him out of uniform, he had a drink in his hand.

"Darrin! Kathy! Elmer! Come in!"

He never would have broken protocol to call us by our first names while in uniform, but this was not work. We were not in uniform, and his drink had already loosened his usual workplace formality.

He led us in. "The drinks and food are over there, and the pool and Jacuzzi are out back, but let me show you around first."

He held me firmly with his arm around my shoulders and led me on my personal tour, finally arriving in what I would call his living room. A beautiful, shiny, black full-grand piano sat in the center. The keys moved without fingers to depress them and beautiful melodies floated from the open lid.

Joan sat on the piano bench swaying to the music, hypnotized by the movement of the keys amidst the din of a very lively party.

Her hair was unrestrained. I'd never seen it at full length. I had never even seen her without scrubs on. I stood and watched from behind. Kathy and Elmer moved on through the house. I don't know how long I'd clandestinely observed her, but suddenly I was shoved forcefully out the back door to the patio. Kathy obviously felt I had reached my time limit. "Come on," she said. "It's getting a little weird."

Dusk was already falling as we arrived in the back yard. The sinking sun cast long tortuous shadows through the twisted and knurled scrub oak trees. In the foreground was a large Jacuzzi with a waterfall that plunged into a pool just beyond it, and in the distance was a fairway I occasionally played golf on—one of the most picturesque and exclusive clubs in the area. The air was warm and sultry as befitting a Central Texas in July—absolutely perfect. The clear blue pool beckoned. Several residents who had obviously begun drinking earlier—finally loosed for a moment from the constraints of their grueling military medicine residency—were playing chicken in the pool, screaming and giggling as they drunkenly careened into one another, splashing everyone within range. One of the revelers was Gisselle, a second year resident from the island of Tobago. Petite, dark skinned, dark haired, and absolutely stunning. In direct contrast to Joan, she was also flirtatious, somewhat crass, foul mouthed, and married. Just my type—at least what had *been* my type. Prior to meeting Joan, I'd contemplated initiating an affair with her—a move that could easily have gotten me removed from the Air Force, or even killed considering Gisselle's husband had recently been charged in a court of law for shooting and killing a neighbor's noisy pet dog. No matter the consequences, though, I would have, with enough time, given a tryst my best shot. Consequences were future events. I was comfortably living in the present. No hint of the mores of my childhood.

That night, I registered Gisselle was still beautiful, especially in a bikini, but thought nothing more about her. My attraction to Joan was overwhelming.

Kathy, Elmer, and I stood nursing our drinks at a safe distance from Joan. She was now standing beneath one of the scrub oaks amiably conversing with another resident, wearing khaki shorts and a hippyish, knit, three quarter sleeved, V-necked blouse with small earth-toned horizontal zigzag stripes. Her shorts were short enough to show off her long slender thighs, but long enough to leave the alluring rest to my imagination. Her blouse clung to her breasts and—without being revealing—accentuated their weight and suppleness as they rose toward her graceful neck. I was absolutely enthralled by her perfect posture, the fluid way in which she moved, and most of all, the way in which she drew people close to her without seeming effort. She was never alone that night. As she stood in the same place beneath her tree, it seemed each of the guests stopped to talk with her at least once. I imagined each left feeling like they were the most important person on the planet.

"Kath. Elm. She's beautiful."

Kathy tried to bring me back to reality. "She's too good for you."

"Do you see how other people are attracted to her?"

"Yeah, she's an irresistible force."

And then Elmer spoke. "You shouldn't ask her out Darrin. She's the marryin' kind."

Despite Elmer's warning, later that night, I approached Joan and asked her to accompany us to a local bar. I didn't go anywhere without Kath and Elm, and I was sure this bar would appeal to the sort of hippy alternative girl I perceived her to be. Joan politely but immediately declined—no explanation.

Dumbfounded—not at all used to my affections being rebuffed, I hesitated. By the slight empathetic crinkle at the outside of her eyes, I knew she'd caught my disappointment.

"Then how about tomorrow night?" I asked.

Her eyes squinted differently at the corners. "Sorry, I have a prior commitment."

I thought, *Dammit! What is wrong with her?*

Then she offered an olive branch. "Maybe we could meet on Thursday at the Black Eyed Pea?"

4

"I Think I Like You, Darrin Dixon"

The Black Eyed Pea was not my idea of a proper venue for such an important first date. It was, and still is, a Southernish cafeteria-style restaurant. A chain whose specialty, as I recall, was fried fish, greasy hushpuppies, and sautéed greens with a generous helping of pecan pie. I liked all of those things, but I was slightly put off by her choice. Fancying myself somewhat of a gourmet cook, I was a proud graduate of several impressive cooking courses and turned my nose up at the thought of taking such a fine woman to a restaurant with such lowly fare. Joan's choice left me wondering about her taste in food and, of course, I easily extrapolated her lack of culinary acumen to the rest of her life. Maybe I had misjudged her.

My entry into cooking as a teenager had been culinary self-pres-ervation—both of my parents worked, and I loved food enough to learn to fend for myself. Mostly, though, I surmised even at an early age that women would be attracted to a man who could cook, so I learned. I didn't start with simple recipes. One of my first desserts—crème puffs made from scratch. Filling and all. I was particularly proud of that dessert, my family loved it, and so did my girlfriend and her family. I had already been proven correct that "chicks would dig it" on many occasions, but Joan wasn't following the usual script.

The restaurant was near the Medical Center in a very busy area of San Antonio. The building was unimpressive, and the parking lot was barely half full as I drove in—a bad sign for a restaurant in my estimation. I parked and got out of my car, walking toward the entrance with a sense of haughty distaste. What I didn't know was that she had chosen this restaurant because it was quite public—she was somewhat wary of my reputation. The building was also very close to her apartment, something I found out later. She was much too busy in her first year of residency to spend an hour driving to what I would have deemed an appropriate dining establishment.

Out of the corner of my eye, I caught sight of her long, olive colored legs shod only in Birkenstocks sliding out of a black Saab 900. I hated Saabs. The car, even though new, looked like a little bubble on wheels. Our first date was going from bad to worse, and I hadn't even greeted her yet. As I began to second guess my feelings about Joan, I did register that she may have arrived early and been waiting for me. Was she as anxious as I was?

We said hello awkwardly without touching.

Joan wore a t-shirt with a picture of Mickey Mouse on the front and a pair of jean shorts. Somehow the shirt looked as if it was custom made, accentuating her long graceful neck and feminine shoulders. Her hair cascaded down almost to the belt line of her shorts, and her only adornment was a French manicure visible on the toes sticking out of her fashionably hippyish Birkenstocks. Even dressed down, she was beautiful and surprisingly sexy in that sort of Midwestern way that I thought I had left behind. Joan wasn't fair haired like the women of Dutch heritage back home, but she wore very little makeup, had a modest hair style, and a simple, innocent, and familiar glow. I wore a pair of khaki cargo shorts and a faded golf shirt—somewhere between grunge and preppy. I still hadn't pegged her style and wanted room to maneuver.

From the moment she spoke her first word of greeting, I forgot about the building and its décor. I have no memory of the inside. I don't recall if it was full or empty. I can't for the life of me remember the carpet or type of chairs. What hung on the walls? I don't know. I don't even remember what I had for dinner or what Joan may have had. I was so engrossed in the fascinating human being before me that everything else was completely eclipsed. She was indeed everything I felt I should want in a mate.

We talked about our families. We talked about our jobs. We discussed every subject that came to our minds. We could have been sitting at our table or booth for hours or days. The next thing I remember, we were standing in the parking lot beside Joan's car and I was kissing her cheek chastely as we said goodnight. I caught the faint hint of fresh soap and butterscotch and managed to whisper, "Can I see you again?"

Her cheery reply, "Oh, yes. I would love that."

We exchanged phone numbers.

"Should I call you? I don't want to go through the torture of wondering if you're going to call."

Her eyes lit up and crinkled at the corners. Her mouth widened into a big grin.

"Yes, pleeease. I think I like you, Darrin Dixon."

She said my name. The impact of hearing the two words that encompassed the whole of who I was out of the mouth of someone I had just fallen head-over-heels in love with was like an atomic bomb exploding in my limbic system. It was our first date, and already I sensed that Joan knew everything she needed to know about me. The way she peered deeply into my eyes without being intrusive, the way we seemed to somehow share energy as skin touched skin. Everything about her screamed that she was being genuine, that she truly accepted me as the man I was and the man I someday hoped to be, that she divined every atom of good within me. All without really knowing me.

[5]

Conversion

Joan and I began to see each other regularly, and I quickly found that she liked a home cooked meal. Joan was actually a closet gourmet with a crunchy, hippy twist. I began to get a bead on her tastes when I learned about Molly Katzen, an idol of Joan's. This idol lived in a commune on the West Coast. At least that's the impression I had. I envisioned Molly as a barefoot, organic, tree hugging chef clad in hemp clothing with a do-rag on her head. Molly wasn't necessarily vegetarian, but she trended toward healthy-ish, ethnic, mostly vegetarian cooking. Raised Seventh Day Adventist, Joan did, too. Having grown up in the center of cattle and pig country, I had never really been exposed to vegetarians, but I took up the challenge of cooking without meat with gusto.

We spent hours every evening—while Joan should have been

studying—standing in the kitchen cooking and experimenting with different recipes. We became closer by the simple act of preparing food together. Joan was the mixer, and I was the chopper. She always put on the finishing touches. We also sampled wine. Joan had never tasted wine, so I introduced her to some of the finer bottles I'd procured over time. We sipped while we cooked. She didn't love the taste, and drinking alcohol—which was forbidden by the same Adventist rules that made Joan's family vegetarian—made her feel just a tiny bit naughty. But she loved the act of drinking wine, the meaning and complexity behind it.

The way Joan felt about wine told me a lot about her. She loved things with meaning. She loved to think and discuss things that mattered. She was also somewhat adventurous and didn't mind questioning some of her church's "minor" beliefs/dogma, such as its Levitical dietary laws from the Bible. One of the church's founders, Ellen White, was said to have received visions from God concerning healthy living and eating. Visions were suspect in the Baptist church I grew up in. We'd been taught there'd be no more visions given by God in our lifetimes. I knew absolutely nothing about Adventists prior to meeting Joan and was nowhere near religious at the time, but had always enjoyed learning about new things, so I threw myself into researching her religion.

I soon learned that Seventh Day Adventists took the fourth commandment in the Bible literally—as did the Jews—and so worshipped on the seventh day, Saturday, as prescribed. They believe that Sunday worship came about as an edict by Constantine in the year A.D. 321 as an attempt to make worshipping a Christian God more attractive to pagans. Sabbath was not what she considered a minor belief. In fact, she believed—as did the rest of the Seventh Day Adventists— that attending church on the Holy Sabbath Day was what set them apart from the other Christian religions and identified them as God's chosen people or the "remnant church" that will stand with God in the end times. She did not go out on Sabbath, a day she reserved for God and family as well as the reason she declined my first invitation—and in this way, she set herself apart. If she sometimes felt left out for holding to her beliefs, she never once bowed to pressure from the outside world—something I was highly attracted to, but had no experience with. My "beliefs" were more... fluid.

As a child growing up in the Baptist church, I'd been trained in Bible study and taught that the Bible was the holy and literal word of God. And I still believed it. Even if I wasn't ready to make a firm commitment to God, I was comfortable talking about religion with Joan and came across as much more intimate with Him than I felt. The truth was that the church was a place I'd always been dragged to—a duty, not a privilege like I'd been taught, a privilege those poor people in China didn't have. Church was where I was forced to dress up in my tiny little homemade (by my mom), three-piece, green plaid suit; a place where a holy man stood behind a podium pointing his finger at me; a place where the sermon was either too boring to possibly stay awake—which elicited a swat on the back of the head from my mother or a neighbor—or a place where I was harangued with hell fire and brimstone, told I was a sinner, and assured that I was going to hell if I didn't change my ways. With the exception of my few return trips home to see family, I hadn't been in a church for years. And yet, I enjoyed going with Joan.

The first church we attended together was Joan's Sabbath church. It was quite small. The very first time I attended, I had just had knee surgery and was on crutches. Joan insisted we sit in the front pew because she was the pianist. At one point in the service, the pastor asked the audience to kneel and pray. My internal dialogue went like this:

"Kneel? Is he crazy? I can't kneel."

"But I have to kneel. I'm at the front of the church, and the freaking pianist is my girlfriend."

"Who kneels in church? I have twenty years of religion under my belt, and I have never had to kneel."

"Are these people Catholic?"

Her church was not so very different than the one I had grown up in. People dressed conservatively. The layout was the same—a stage with a podium in front, a choir loft behind, a baptistery behind that. An organ was stage right and the piano, which Joan played, was stage left. The church building itself was small and utilitarian. Later, at lunch, Joan whispered her secret belief that many Adventist churches hadn't been built with much thought because Adventists believed we were living in the very end of times. Why would you build an expensive church when Jesus was soon to appear? Baptists also believed we were living in the end times, but we were too proud to skimp on building materials. The pastor gave the same sermon I'd heard a million times, we sang the same hymns, and we stayed for the same potluck meal after church with the same old ladies stuffing their oversized purses with goodies to take home. I could have been at my old church except for the fact that it was Saturday, the food was all vegetarian, and I was missing college football.

Joan and I were both raised in very strict middle class households that believed in strong Christian values like grace, faith, hope, love, justice, joy, service, and peace. The only differences seemed to be that Joan had somehow learned those many lessons and taken them to heart. Not my parent's fault that I hadn't—they taught me how they had been taught. They'd taken me to church faithfully (my father attending as an unspoken stipulation of his marriage to my mother), and they introduced me to the Bible, but I always felt they struggled with the same issue I did—how to interpret all the dogma and make God real. Each Sunday, we attended Sunday school and then church in the morning and again in the evening. Frequently, we also attended Wednesday evening prayer meeting and always a youth program named AWANA (Approved Workmen Are Not Ashamed)—an attempt by the church to make learning Bible verses fun and exciting with an added bit of competition for global appeal that seemed to me not very Biblical. My parents were even the leaders. But the only time I had ever felt God as a living breathing being to whom I could actually speak and listen to was one brief moment as a twelve-year-old. That night, a visiting evangelist was speaking at our church. I have long forgotten his name and his words, but I vividly recall how I could—for the first time—feel the Holy Spirit I had heard so much about. An overwhelming burst of emotion, a torrent of depth and gravity swept over me, and I suddenly glimpsed how small I really was—how big my Savior was. The organist played "Just As I Am," and the evangelist gave his alter call, one I had heard countless times. This night, my body moved without conscious thought. I was drawn to the front of the sanctuary before I even opened my eyes. The Spirit took over my body and propelled me forward, guided me to the front. Minutes later in the dark back hallway behind the stage, Lawrence Kingery, already stooped and wrinkled with age, placed his hand on my shoulder. I could feel him tremble, but there was strength in his firm grip that I recognized as otherworldly. Tears slipped down my face, and when I looked up, his cheeks glistened with his own. He read from the Book of Romans, then asked, "Are you ready to let Jesus into your heart, son? Are you ready to change your life?" Without hesitation, sobbing and on my knees, I said, "Yes."

Within a month of that day that held so much gravity, I was groping some easy girl in the back seat of her car—I was much too young to drive—and taking my first drink of Southern Comfort while watching soft core porn in the basement of my friend's house while his parents were sleeping—bringing myself to a clumsy orgasm beneath the sheets on the couch after the lights were turned out. Hoping desperately not to be discovered, I'd found myself powerless over my adolescent desires, unable to deny myself that sinful release.

My feeling of "sinfulness" was quickly forgotten as I found myself with ever growing opportunities to experiment with older girls in high school. Far from feeling sinful, sex became fun and fascinating as I began college in halfhearted pursuit of a career in art. Having given up my childhood dreams of military glory as inconvenient, I had moved out of the restrictive confines of my parents' house and out of the barren fields of my small town to the land of plenty in the big city and college with open minded artists. Church became a thing that younger kids and older adults did. God was relegated to an image I would revisit someday.

Though I should have been having the time of my life, something wasn't working. I began skipping classes, isolating myself, and feeling less and less enamored of my life.

I don't know where I would have ended up, but my mother, a nurse, became aware that I was struggling. Though I was living away from home, she recognized my detachment and aimlessness over the phone. She also kept tabs on my grades and knew my heart wasn't in art school. She knew nothing of my lifestyle. Out of the blue, she suggested I follow a friend of hers to explore nurse anesthesia as a possible vocation. I fell in love with a calling that encompassed both hard science and the art of understanding each distinct human being and the differences in each intricate system.

I signed up for a two-year nursing school. I worked my way through my associate's degree in nursing at the parts counter at Sears, and then after attaining my RN, I worked the evening shift in an ICU to pay my way through the last two years of my bachelor's degree. I rekindled my past dreams and joined the Air Force after graduation because their anesthesia program was ranked in the top five in the nation. I chose San Antonio because that was where the Air Force anesthesia school was located. As soon as I was settled into the Air Force, I sought and was accepted into the University of Texas Health Science Center where I began taking master's classes that would bolster my resume when I submitted my package to the Air Force anesthesia program. I applied for my scholarship a year earlier than allowed in hopes that—though they would be forced to turn me down—the selection board would see my name and recognize it the next year. By chance, or good planning, two weeks before classes started, in the year before I was officially allowed to seek acceptance, I received a call telling me that someone had dropped out of the program days before they were supposed to begin—something I could scarcely have dreamed of—and because I was the top applicant, asked me if I was prepared to start. I was.

Though I had joined the Air Force for selfish reasons, somewhere between joining and the year after I graduated from my anesthesia program, I realized I had gained love for my country and a fierce feeling of protection for her people. The feeling didn't come in a great crashing wave. I just woke up one day and realized that I'd become the patriot I'd been as a seven-year-old marching in a homemade civil war costume in my local parade.

But even with my newfound patriotism, I still worshiped at the church of self. A bar or dance club was my place of worship—a place to hang out with other sinners without judgement, a place to meet someone to take me in her arms and love me for who I was that night, not who I was supposed to be.

It wasn't that I didn't want to commune with the God of my parents, or that I didn't want to become a "good" person, or even that I didn't want to turn my entire life around and begin serving the Lord. In fact, I desired those things very much. But I still identified with St. Augustine's lament: "Lord give me chastity and sobriety, but just not yet!" I felt I needed more time to give up my lifestyle for something as nebulous as a Being I couldn't see or hear.

That Sabbath with Joan was my first and last experience in her Saturday (Sabbath) church. Joan's too. We found her Sunday place of worship was more my style, though we still kept Saturday as a Sabbath at home. Max Lucado's church was nondenominational and much less conservative. Max was a prolific Christian author and rock star for Jesus. My mom even knew about him. His membership was larger and seemed to be less judgmental than Joan's. The Oak Hills church put on several services, so we didn't have to get up early. It also had interesting speakers. I had gotten my fill of rhetoric and judgement as a child. I began to hope that I'd found a church where I would be accepted, where I could begin to build my own relationship with God in my own way.

The one thing I didn't expect was the depth of Joan's goodness.

I surreptitiously watched her at work. She was loving with everyone.

———

The "two striper" nicknamed "Sloopy" was one of her favorites. He was funny, smart, hardworking, and caring. He was also very poor. At the age of 25—which was our age—he already had four children. He was very close to the bottom of the totem pole in the Air Force and relied on food stamps to buy groceries to feed his children and wife. Joan worked with him in the preoperative clinic. He was the front desk worker who delivered the chart to the provider and called the patient's name when it was their time to be seen. Sloopy was never given a break for lunch. Others who worked the desk either made time or brought food with them to eat on the run. Sloopy never took the time to go to the cafeteria, and he never brought a lunch. All his money went to feeding and clothing his children. Joan intuitively knew this and secretly brought treats for him to "try out" under the guise of being her taste tester. He gladly ate everything she brought. The charade continued until he was transferred to another unit.

Joan also spent time—time she didn't have—volunteering at a mission. She served dinner there as often as she could. She crocheted little things for bedside tables and painted positive sayings in calligraphy on the walls of the little rooms the residents called home. It was a dirty place. She swept the floors and scrubbed the bathrooms.

She spent money she hadn't yet accumulated to support a children's home.

Her favorite child was a girl named Naomi. I accompanied Joan there once. The people at the front desk knew Joan by sight.

As we walked in, the woman at the front said, "Hi, Joan."

She hadn't told them she was a doctor.

"Naomi is in the play room. I'll go get her."

The moment the child was in her arms, Joan forgot about me.

She was transformed—and so was the child—as if a bubble surrounded and insulated them from the outside world. I could only watch from the corner, amazed at their conversion, overlooking for the moment that she had forgotten about me.

And yet, I hadn't forgotten about me. Joan's goodness soon became overwhelming to me. She began to take on the role of my parents in a subtle but eerie way. She was becoming my new moral compass—something to live up to. Something to be judged by? I didn't yet know, but I began to feel ill at ease with my past and remained continually on my guard—acting as if I were comfortable with her spiritual things, but secretly not being comfortable at all. I couldn't help but wonder how she would respond to the very different ways we had lived our lives.

My Personal Hero

Barely settled back into a routine in San Antonio after Honduras, I was sent by Colonel Kelly to Air Force flight nursing school. I arrived at Brooks Air Force base, ten miles across town, in a foul mood. Tired of being away from home, knowing I would be living in a dorm for the next six weeks, missing Joan, I thought flight nursing school was a waste of my time. As far as I was concerned, flight nurses were a bunch of clipboard carrying, middle management bureaucrats who couldn't think outside of any script. I was the direct antithesis of them. My entire life was off script. I had done so well in the military because I could accomplish anything put before me, not because I followed the rules.

Colonel Kelly felt differently than I. He saw the six-week long school as career enhancement. He knew having knowledge of the air evacuation system would make me valuable to some of the units he was trying to get me into. Apparently, the Joint Special Operations Command was smarter than I was, too. They sent Steve.

I was 6'1" and weighed 200 pounds, but Steve towered over me. Clearly athletic—his swagger and fluid nimble movements proved it—he had massive shoulders and thighs that strained the material of his uniform, a red beret perched jauntily on his shortly cropped hair, and green pants bloused at the bottom and tucked into a pair of jump boots—the uniform of an Army paratrooper. His left chest was completely filled with ribbons and the shiny metal badges I so coveted—all with the wreath around them signifying they had been earned in actual combat. On his right sleeve was the gold-and-black ace of spades patch identifying him as a member of US Special Operations Command. His jaw was clenched, and his chin jutted forward strongly. His eyes were vigilant, evaluating everyone who came near. He was a giant.

Each step I moved closer to him, I fell more deeply in awe. There in front of me was a living breathing example of everything I had worked so diligently to become. I couldn't believe my luck.

"Hi, I'm Captain Dixon."

"I'm Steve."

Steve was a major and I could tell he was older than me, but not how much. Fishing on with small talk, I assessed him. He returned the favor. We danced slowly—him with a friendly, still, politeness and me doing the best I could to maintain my composure in the presence of my new hero.

"What brings you here, Steve?"

"Oh, I had a couple of months off and thought this would be interesting."

To myself I thought, "A couple of months off? What in the hell is he talking about? The military only allows thirty days off a year and he 'had a couple of months off?'" I needed this life. Needed it like oxygen.

"How do you get a couple of months off? Does the Army have a new policy? I'm here because my boss wants me to be the DG (distinguished graduate). He's bound and determined to make me a colonel, too."

"No, the Army doesn't have a new policy. The people I work for think it would be good for us to know the ins and outs of the Air Force Air Evacuation System."

"The current system is kind of a joke. If our patient is too sick, Air Evac won't take them."

"Yeah, that's the problem we're running into. Most of our patients are pretty seriously injured, and Air Evac won't accept them."

I wondered if Steve was a part of a certain classified group. The holy grail for me. Not wanting to ruin my chance to get close to him by endangering operational security on the very day that I met him, I said carefully. "I'm going to say some letters and you tell me if they mean anything to you: J-M-O."

"Yeah, that's it, but you're spelling it wrong."

Inside my head I thought, *Fantastic. I'm trying to be cool and secretive to show him I am worthy of his respect, and I fuck up by spelling his group wrong. Dumb ass.* Definitely not the way I wanted to make an impression, but Steve chuckled aloud.

Whatever I had done seemed to work. We sat in the back of the classroom every day and made fun of the incredibly stupid and restrictive rules that governed air evac nursing. Steve and I were the cocks of the walk in a class filled with young female technicians and nurses. Two of the only men in the course, and we both stood out as extraordinary. Neither of us minded being popular.

"Steve, do you think two of these 115 pound nurses can lift an Army Ranger with full gear over their heads to the top stretcher rest?"

"Let's see!"

Steve suggested to the instructors that he and I lie on the stretchers and be lifted by the nurses to simulate actual circumstances. The instructors pursed their lips and squinted their eyes, but in the end allowed us to play. But Steve hadn't thought about the very real probability that one or both of us would be dropped flat on our backs on the ground when the nurse's arms failed. We took a few hard landings.

On our off duty time, Steve and I exercised incessantly, running and lifting weights. He was built like a brick shit house and was stronger than anyone I had ever been near. He oozed testosterone, drawing women to him as moths to a flame. When we weren't exercising or flirting, we spent our time in our dorms together polishing our boots and discussing myriad topics. Steve was smart, he was strong, he was ambitious. He had an ironical laid back air with an underlying intensity.

We became buddies and more over the course of six weeks with all of the time together in class, in the officer's club, exercising, and trying to sleep with as many of the nurses as we could. He seemed to have it all, and I fell under his spell, though I did my very best not to show my idol worship to Steve or any of the women we were around. He knew. Steve was not only in the group I longed to be a part of, but he lived the way I did in the curious military fashion that we had become accustomed to. He was hard charging, hardworking, hard living while away, but maintained a loving wife and children at home. I wondered how he pulled it off.

Toward the end of the six weeks, Steve told me his wife's birthday was the next weekend and she was traveling to San Antonio to celebrate. He invited me to come along with a companion. We ate, got drunk, got good and aroused (Steve and his wife oozed sex, my female partner almost as much), danced, were publicly indecent, and then retired to a luxury suite and a very large bed for the four of us.

Twenty-four hours a day, seven days a week, for six weeks, I lived with a real life example of my personal dream. We even bonded in a tattoo parlor for four hours as Steve sat with a dark mixture of blood and ink oozing from his hip during a tattoo application. On a whim fueled by a mixture of boredom and heady connection to Steve, I watched as a clamp was applied to my left nipple and a large needle passed through—a small silver bar replacing it—something Joan merely nodded her head at and said "hmm" with her slightly pursed lips when she discovered it weeks later.

I returned from flight school spent from my weekend with Steve, his wife, and my "friend," as well as from three days of survival school in the "wilderness" of Central Texas. The survival wasn't the tiring part. The nurse on each side of me each night attempting to stay warm was.

I fell back into Joan's arms with a new purpose, dedicated to giving my new mentor Steve's dual life a try. Immediately upon returning to work, Colonel Kelly sent me on another "career enhancing" TDY, this time to Squadron Officer's School in Montgomery, Alabama. Joan and I struggled to see each other in the small amount of time between Flight School and SOS. I easily slipped back into my old ways as soon as I left town.

One beautiful fall afternoon, I was hitting a volleyball around with another captain when someone strode confidently up to me. I sensed a not-so-subtle seductiveness as she came to a stop with her breasts touching my chest. Her scent was sweet and slightly salty with perspiration as she peered up at me and spoke. Small, but incredibly fit, her hair was kinky curly, even pinned up within Air Force regulation 35-10 that governed our appearance. Through our PT uniforms—that were of course Air Force blue shorts and a t-shirt—I could feel the tautness of her sports bra as she took slow, even breaths.

"My name is Cindy. You can call me Sin..." She paused to let that sink in, then continued, "This is my roommate, best friend, and fellow helicopter pilot. Her sister is a porn star."

"I'm Darrin. That's the most interesting introduction I've ever heard. I think I'm in love. I like your roommate, too."

"Let's play volleyball."

Sin played a good game of volleyball. She also lived up to her name. And my dreams of having Joan at home waiting while I was on TDY seemed that much more realistic.

The Thanksgiving holiday approached. Steve and his wife, who were stationed within driving distance of SOS, graciously invited me to visit.

Their kids were strangely absent throughout my entire weekend with them. I know they were there, but I remember nothing about them. "Dinner" began each afternoon with drinks. Drambuie and Butterscotch Schnapps on the rocks for a quick hit, then on to Killian's Irish Red or Chimay while we made and ate homemade salsa and chips. I think we grilled steaks and potatoes on the barbecue one day, but that became lost in the haze of alcohol and later events.

The weather was cool, but I felt a pleasant warm glow from the alcohol, the presence of a man I admired, a woman I was attracted to, and the memory of another time together. As we shed our clothes and stepped into the hot tub, my heart raced, but I remained calm on the outside. I always did. We weren't shy. There was no reason to be. She was sexy. She was even sexier with Steve right next to us. I am fully heterosexual, but Steve was so overwhelmingly manly, I couldn't help but be strangely attracted to him.

She said, "You seem like you have something on your mind, Sexy."

My reply: "More than you know…"

"Do you want to talk about it?"

"Maybe after a while."

She came closer. "Maybe after this?"

She kissed me firmly on the lips, forcing her tongue into my mouth. Her hand came to my left nipple, the one I had pierced while Steve got his tattoo. Her nipples were pierced too—both. A hand slid down my belly.

"Yeah, maybe after this," I said huskily.

Her mouth followed her hands. I knew he was watching. I closed my eyes, trying to stay in the moment, tantalizingly close to orgasm, but I hung there, just on the edge.

Their children were somewhere above sleeping. At least I desperately hoped they were sleeping. What was I doing? Silently: *This is insane. Sex is one thing. Sex with the wife of a man I admire with him watching, another. Sex in their hot tub in their back yard with their young children one level above us, quite possibly watching their mother give me a blow job, is too much.* Dizzy in my depravity, every dirty little deed I had done in the last several years suddenly rushed through my mind and I knew I had finally gone too far. In that moment, I knew that Joan was my future and that together, we had so much more than this furtive dual life. We connected on a deeper level. We were meant for each other. We had a future.

I had expected my "St. Augustine" moment would come someday. I just hadn't expected it in the middle of a hot tub, naked, with another man and his wife.

7

Good Girl

Though I maintained my own apartment after returning to San Antonio, Joan and I spent most of our evening and nights together. We slept together, but without consummating our relationship. I was quite sure she was still a virgin, and while this might have aroused me at another time with someone else, now I only felt admiration and a certain longing for a future time. Though I felt myself changing merely from being near Joan, I still didn't trust my motives. I worried that I would lose interest soon after I "conquered" her. I couldn't bring myself to debauch her and then leave her. I was trying desperately to live up to my parents' ideals, which were similar to Joan's ideals, which were slowly becoming my ideals again.

One night we lay on Joan's apartment floor casually touching and caressing while we talked about our day, or our families, maybe even work. As she playfully twirled the hair on my chest through the "v" in my shirt, I naturally became aroused. "Are you trying to torture me?" I said with a false sense of agony.

"Torture? Hardly." Her hand slid down from its perch on my chest to my waistline. "You don't seem too tormented. Did you know your brain is your most important sex organ?" Her hand slid lower still from my belt to my thigh, then slowly, excruciatingly upward again, until it rested with her fingers between my legs. "Do you know there are 4,000 nerve endings in the glans of the penis?"

Only a doctor would use the medical term "glans" in sex talk.

I said, "Umm, no, I'm not sure I believe you. Could you demonstrate?"

With a come hither look she said, "Let's see. How would I do that?"

"I'll leave that part up to you."

She continued on with her anatomy lesson. "Oh yeah, did you know the clitoris has double that amount."

She said it proudly, as if this proved her superior as a woman.

"I had no idea. Maybe we could construct a study to prove your theory."

"A study might be fun."

I pulled her head closer to mine and kissed her. My hand slid down past her ear, hesitating by the side of her graceful neck before moving lower, just barely brushing her left breast and coming to a stop on her hip.

Joan was hesitant.

"There's something that I've been meaning to tell you."

"That you're a virgin?"

"Is it that obvious?"

"Not obvious."

"What do you think?"

"I'm in awe of your restraint. I admire you."

"It's not just being a 'good girl.' I've dreamt of my wedding night since I was five years old. I want it to be perfect. I want the fairy tale."

"Then you shall have your fairy tale."

I knew there was a good man, a man my parents would be proud of, a man Joan could respect, hidden somewhere inside of me, and I was suddenly proud of that one small step I'd taken. I felt like I was finally becoming the man who could erase those wrongs from my childhood—being thrown out of vacation Bible school, being kicked out of school for fighting, losing my virginity in a clumsy, adolescent flurry on the front seat of an orange Chevy Nova after a basketball game, taking another's virginity on a cool fall night in the prickly hay, stealing furniture for my boss, racking up a list of dozens of adult women, some at the same time, lying, scheming, fighting. I wondered if Joan would still view me as her knight in shining armor if she knew the full extent of my trespasses. She'd been taught the same definition of sin as I had. I would have no fairy tale first time on my wedding night—at least not in the way that Joan would. I had strayed too far and couldn't get over the feeling that God would surely punish me in some way.

"You know I'm not a virgin, don't you?"

"You are who you are. You've done what you've done. I accept you as you."

Through my head passed the words, "God, I love you."

8

The Ring

Spring arrived in Central Texas, and with the blooming of the wildflowers, I was finally ready to admit to others that I was in love. My best friend, Mike, from my early Air Force career was the first person to hear me say the words; my other best friend, Kathy, was the second; Joan was third. I'd known Mike the longest. We had lost touch slightly as I went through anesthesia school and residency and he completed his nursing degree, but we would always share a special bond, even to this day.

The morning I told Mike was a particularly beautiful day in San Antonio. It was mid-spring, and the temperature was in the seventies. The citywide celebration of Fiesta was just a few days away. There were few clouds in the sky as we sat at a table in front of our Starbucks in an outdoor mall on the west side of the large city. The setting wasn't intimate, but by then, our mutual friendship rendered setting inconsequential. I sipped my mocha and narrowed my eyes. Mike knew by my expression that something big was coming.

"Dude, I love her."

"What did you say?"

"I'm in love."

"Get the fuck out of here."

"Serious, man."

Mike accompanied me on my quest to find the perfect jeweler to create the perfect ring for Joan, and we ended up visiting at least a dozen before we found the right creative force. Any one of the various shops probably would have worked as well as the one I settled on, but I wanted this ring to be perfect. And besides, Mike and I were having such a good time being together again that we just kept looking.

Mike kept repeating, "Dude, you're different. I can't believe it."

I kept repeating, "Wait until you get to know her better. You'll understand."

Before I could even give her the ring, Joan's usual calm positive outlook took a dark turn. She was an anesthesia resident in a time of severe shortage of young doctors. The residents worked to exhaustion and were highly stressed, pushed to maintain the same output, collectively, as if their residency were at full capacity. Joan became more withdrawn and demoralized in her exhaustion, and as she withdrew, she was soon singled out as an underachiever.

Having previously attended more accommodating Christian schools, Joan had arrived at Wilford Hall ill prepared for the rigors of a military medicine residency. She always seemed a little lost and slightly behind in the chaos of the daily operating room schedule. I couldn't decide if her confusion was due to what I imagined as softer training in medical school or her gentle personality. Her stubborn unwillingness to complete tasks without questioning their utility earned her the label "lazy" which was paramount to death to a first year resident, something I wasn't sure she'd recover from. She was hurt and demoralized when she caught on that her staff and peers felt this way. With me as a part of the staff that wasn't making her life any easier, we were soon at odds.

Nights of cooking together, reading together, and talking until we fell asleep became more like nights of getting takeout on our way home, eating in silence, then watching Joan escape to bed. I even began sleeping in my own apartment again. Whenever we did talk, Joan complained incessantly, especially about Giselle who—after I'd let go of my aspirations for an affair—had become a friend. Giselle was still flirtatious with me—she was flirtatious with any male, especially if she believed she could gain something from them. She had also become a very well respected senior resident. Joan hated her.

Joan hated her because Giselle was smart, charismatic, and played her part in the everyday schedule. The female anesthesiologists tended to like those qualities. The males… well, the males simply found her captivating. I was one of them. Gisselle used the gifts she had been given, including dancing the new Macarena in the middle of presenting a case gone wrong at our department's morbidity and mortality conference in front of sixty staff and residents. She got an easy ride. Joan wouldn't have deigned to use her looks or charm to pave her way to an easier three years. She was above that type of behavior. I didn't understand.

The softness I'd found endearing as I courted her now troubled me. Why didn't she use her unbelievable gifts of charm, intelligence, even beauty to manipulate her way through? Instead she passive-aggressively connived to get out of work even if it meant one of her classmates would have to pick up her slack. She was on the verge of quitting so many times, only to be pulled back from the brink with a timely pep talk by dear old Kathy who had become her lifeline and friend. I began to harbor doubts. If she couldn't complete a three-year residency, how could she carry through on a lifelong commitment like marriage?

Things might have ended there, but one evening, I returned home from work later than Joan. The apartment was dark. I didn't call her name for fear she was sleeping—something she was doing more and more of. The bedroom door was open, but the room was dark inside—drapes drawn. Joan loved the light, so a sense of dread crept over me as I walked to the open door and peered inside. She was lying on her right side atop her covers in a fetal position, eyes open, yet unfocused. As she peered absently toward the ceiling, I could see she was far away. Joan had a very active fantasy life. I wondered briefly if she was there, in her Disney fantasy world, but quickly realized she inhabited a much darker place. Her lips did not smile as they did when she was with Mickey.

"Joan?"

No answer. I had never seen her this way before. "Joanie?"

She loved when I called her Joanie. I suddenly realized how much I loved her. She was wounded, and a desperate need to comfort her rose from within me.

I lay next to her on the bed, curling around her, but not touching her at first. Eventually, I touched her shoulder, and she stirred slightly. I stroked her hair.

She said, "Hi," in a soft, childlike voice. As if I had just arrived.

"Do you want to talk or just lay here for a while?"

"Just lay here."

"I love you."

"I know."

That night, lying side by side, feeling her heart beat, feeling the rise and fall of her chest as she breathed, as tears gently coursed down her cheek and onto my hand, I could feel myself changing. I had never felt a sense of empathy and protectiveness for another human being like the one I experienced lying with Joan. Later, we quietly decided to visit Southern California for her brother's wedding to one of her close friends. The final straw for her this day had been when she was denied leave by her program director to attend the wedding. The denial had sent her into a tailspin that ended in her dark room with the shades drawn. We left for Southern California the next week. Joan went AWOL. She had three days in which she wasn't technically bound to be in the local area. All we had to do was get to Southern California and back before Monday morning when she was supposed to work again.

On the flight, Joan noticeably relaxed. The farther away from San Antonio we traveled, the more at ease she was. We arrived at her brother's house before any of the other guests—notably her mother and father whom we had just found out were divorcing.

I was a little surprised to find we were given our own room—one with two mattresses on the floor, but one room—despite having Joan's mother and father in the same vicinity.

"So, are we going to move them together?" Joan asked. She had a sly little smile on her face—something I'd seen very little of lately.

"Up to you."

"We'll have to move them back apart every morning."

"I suppose we will."

"I don't think I want to sleep clear on the other side of the room from you. I'll be lonely." She shrugged her right shoulder and turned demurely away as she glanced back at me, long eyelashes fluttering.

The next morning, guests began arriving just after breakfast. I hadn't been to a party full of church goers since childhood, but I felt a distant deep memory of the parties after evening church . There was no alcohol, no smoking, no swearing. But there was music, there were games. Not the drinking games I played in college, not the games geared toward getting each other's clothes off, but fun games, boisterous games, innocent games—simpler times.

Wherever Joan was, people gathered. I felt such warmth in her stance and her face. Everyone she was with felt like the luckiest person in the world. I could tell. Just as at the hale and farewell party, she was the sun, the rest of us mere planets, but being near her, we felt like beautiful stars. On her way to and fro, she touched me. Maybe a simple brush as she passed within shoulder length or a kiss on the cheek. She knew without me saying that I was uncomfortable, and she endeavored to lessen my uneasiness. She intuited every emotion in the room. Joan was in her element, and I fell in love again. I was finally ready to give her the ring.

But upon my return to Wilford Hall, Colonel Kelly pulled me into his office.

"You're being reassigned to Osan Air Base, Republic of South Korea, as the chief nurse anesthetist."

I'd become accustomed to Colonel Kelly's kooky ideas about my career, but this came out of the blue.

"That's remote isn't it, Sir?"

"Yes. Twelve months."

"You know Joan and I are getting pretty serious, don't you?"

Joan and I had been secretive about our relationship within the department, but I trusted Colonel Kelly.

"I know. Sit down a minute."

"Yes, Sir."

"You'll have to leave Joanie here. And I need to tell you a couple of things about Korea. I was stationed there once. And for that matter, I need to tell you something about relationships."

"Yes, Sir."

"When you get to Korea, go meet your flight surgeon. Do you want to know why?"

"Yes, Sir."

When Colonel Kelly got going there was little room for two-way communication—only "yessirs" and "nosirs."

"Because one evening, you're going to be sitting around a table at a club outside of base drinking beer. You and your friends are all going to be getting blow jobs under the table at the same time. You're going to need Penicillin."

"Yes, Sir."

"And, when you get your hair cut off-base and they wrap a hot towel around your head, be prepared to get a blow job. It's called "the towel treatment." Whatever you do, don't take the towel off. You never know who is giving you the treatment. It might be the old man barber with no teeth."

I didn't have any idea what to say at that point, so I just kept saying, "Yes, Sir."

"One more thing. If you're married, and you're at home in bed with another woman, and your wife comes in the door to your room, get up. Just get up, put your clothes on, and ask the other woman to leave. If your wife accuses you of sleeping with the other woman, deny it. Even if she caught you red-handed. Deny it. Your denial gives her a reason to doubt."

"Yes, Sir."

By that time, I was frantic to get out of his office before I burst into laughter. I absolutely adored Colonel Kelly, but I didn't know if he was speaking from personal experience or just general knowledge. The last thing I wanted was for him to see me laugh.

I escaped the office without offending him, but instead of asking Joan to marry me prior to leaving Texas for South Korea, I now chose to wait—stowing the beautiful, handmade, custom ring I had designed in a safe deposit box.

[9]

Grace

I arrived at Osan Air Base, Republic of South Korea, to find rampant and accepted infidelity, beautiful Korean and Russian women who were willing to do anything to achieve their life long pass (by marriage) to the United States, sexy and lonely military women in an unsupervised place for the first time in their lives, a college dorm atmosphere with supervisors who were serious about looking the other way, a lot of cheap food and alcohol, and hours and days of mind-numbing boredom and excruciating loneliness. This became clear within minutes of arriving. I'd departed from LAX in the wee hours of the morning. In a military charter with four hundred other soldiers, marines, and airmen, I'd arrived in Seoul somewhere between twelve and fifteen hours later where we boarded a bus that took us the last forty-five minutes to Osan Air Base. I was just off the bus, attempting to come to terms with the fact the entire perimeter of this base was surrounded by razor wire, machine gun nests, and anti-aircraft emplacements. I hadn't imagined my new assignment would be particularly dangerous, but the lethal accouterments gave me pause. I was rethinking my earlier nonchalance as I unpacked my 8x10 portrait of Joan when a knock sounded on the cheap fake wood door. I was surprised and a little irritated because I hadn't slept for nearly twenty-four hours.

I opened the door to find three young, very fit airmen in flight suits and red berets—PJs. After a moment of confused hesitation, Captain Cindy "you can call me Sin" from SOS stepped out from behind the wall of men. I'd forgotten she was going to be rotating through Osan while I was there. I was suddenly uneasy. Cocking her head coquettishly, she said, "Hi."

The four sauntered nonchalantly in. My small dorm room suddenly became uncomfortably crowded.

One of the PJs said, "That's a pretty big picture you have there, Sir."

"Girlfriend."

"She's cute."

"I agree."

With a cocky grin, he said, "Is it to remind you to not screw around?"

My mind was muddled by lack of sleep, the new atmosphere, and my surprise at seeing Sin with three big guys, so I kept my mouth shut.

"Good luck with that…"

Cindy stepped in. "We're staying at the hotel right outside of base. Barbeque on the roof on Sunday if you want to come." She winked as she said it. "Come on boys."

———

Cindy left with her entourage. I remained in my dorm, weary and confused. Was she sleeping with one or all of her "boys?" Did it matter? Was I strong enough to withstand her onslaught if she brought out her big guns? Did I even want to?

That first month, I clung desperately to the idea that I could remain faithful. My phone calls, along with the "poster-sized picture of my girlfriend," were my attempts at holding that line. When I received my first phone bill for over two thousand dollars, I was shocked. The enormous expense became my excuse to stop calling. I effortlessly slid into old destructive behaviors. Alcohol was ever present in Korea, and I partook. Drugs were, too, but I was at least self-aware enough to know the one time I dabbled with them would be the beginning of my never ending quest for more. Sex was for comfort, sex was an outlet for pain when the dark monster inside of me would not be denied, and sex was also my way out of a relationship I felt I could never make good on, an excuse to flee the pressure of becoming that good man my parents had always wanted me to be.

With sex, I was accepted for who I was, not who I was supposed to be, not for who I could be. Merely who I was at that moment. I was smart and athletic to Jill, the cute athletic intel officer I finally manipulated into sleeping with me one afternoon. My first and only attempt at sex with her was clumsy and frenetic—hollow. I orgasmed immediately after I entered her—a first for me since that clumsy night in the orange Nova after our basketball game. Then I made it far worse with Jill by apologizing in defeat. I was kinky and open with Mary, the quirky, new age, alternative officer, who looked like a librarian on the outside, but was stunning naked and unencumbered. We fell into each other's arms on a moral trip put on by the Air Force in the northern part of South Korea. I was trying to get into 's pants at that time, but Mary and I shared a room for convenience. Come to find out, we were both desperately lonely. I was barely able to maintain an erection—for the first time too distracted to really enjoy it. I was an authority figure to the young African American surgical tech who demanded I push her against the wall of my dorm with my hands around her neck while our coworkers were attending a Thanksgiving party just down the hall. While this would have been a turn on for me previously, this time I only felt dirty. A novelty to the Army veterinarian with whom I again failed to perform to my utmost ability, and the great white hope for my Korean girlfriends who couldn't have cared less about how I performed or who I was, only what I bought them. When I distilled my malady down to its core, I found I was hopelessly stricken with an unquenchable thirst for freedom—the freedom to recreate myself, to become whomever I chose without the weight of who I should be. Freedom was much more intoxicating than merely sex, substance, or power. It included all three. I was hopelessly hooked.

I broke up with Joan by email within three months of leaving San Antonio for Korea. No longer worried about Joan's ability to stay true to our relationship, I'd become convinced I was the problem, that I could never live up to her kindness and goodness. Thinking myself free, I was soon missing her. Lonely and lost among a bevy of women, I spiraled into a familiar state of self-absorption which included getting drunk one night on whiskey and espresso and beating an off duty military policeman in a dance club half to death because he was rude to the woman I was dancing with... a woman I barely knew.

My Sunday school teacher was standing at the front of the room. I was on one of the long wooden benches with straight backs and painful slats that I imagined were engineered to keep naughty little children like me awake. Slam went a Bible when my friend and partner in crime, Bobby, became a little too loud and obvious about our shenanigans. "Jesus gave his life for YOUR sins!" Her finger was pointing directly at me, making sure I knew this was personal, and that I was the one responsible for the death of her beloved Jesus. Bobby and I shut up. "Not only did Jesus die on the cross for your sins, but his father, the Almighty God, was forced to send his own Son to be atonement for your sins." I was listening now, trembling with fright, more from her face, so twisted by emotion, than by the words she shouted.

I was similarly frightened when I decided to visit Joan. Having reached bottom, unable to quiet this monster inside of me, I reached out to God. God and Joan where inexorably intertwined for me now. I finally knew there was only one way out of my pain.

I showed up unannounced on her doorstep one morning after a grueling twenty-hour journey from Korea. Joan opened the door and gave a barely perceptible start, then immediately masked it.

"Oh, you're here."

Her open hand covered her mouth as if she had embarrassed herself with her surprise.

"Can we talk?"

"Sure, come in."

I was astonished to find her stronger and seemingly happier than ever. She was already dating someone else (to my horror, a law student named John).

"Do you have a place to stay?" she asked.

Then, I experienced grace. Grace, along with sin, was a concept that had stuck with me from childhood Sunday school. Grace was a manifestation of God's willingness to forgive us humans—sinners—all, and give us clemency, thereby saving our lives and granting us eternal life in Heaven with Him. Joan offered me this same type of grace.

When I told her I hadn't thought that far ahead, she said, "You could stay here."

We were both aware that her invitation was more than just a place to stay.

"What about John?"

"Don't worry about him."

"Are you sure?"

She looked me directly in the eyes. "Are you sure?"

Less than eighteen months later, Joan and I wed in the middle of an intimate, flowered courtyard near a small lake in downtown Orlando, Florida, surrounded by our closest friends and family. I knew I had finally made the right decision, the grown-up decision. Joan lived her fairy tale wedding in the city of her choice—a magical evening in the magical place where Mickey and Minnie Mouse also resided. We spent our first night as a married couple in the small honeymoon suite in a beautiful restored Victorian mansion. A perfect setting for Joan's fairy tale. We had made it worth the wait.

Ten days later, Joan returned to her residency in Texas and I to Macdill Air Force Base in Tampa, Florida. For the next two years— though we were only able to see each other for the occasional weekend or quick anesthesia meeting—I had turned a corner in my mind. After my promises in a courtyard near the lake in Orlando, I no longer felt any temptation to drink or sleep around, even when presented with opportunities. My commitment to Joan held strong, and my addiction to more seemed cured.

Then, as our reunion day drew close, my beloved Air Force challenged our future further. Joan received an assignment to Travis

Air Force Base in Northern California, and I was offered a so-called "joined spouse assignment" to Elmendorf, Alaska because it was within the same command—no matter that it was several thousand miles away. Despite the unofficial Air Force motto of "Semper Gumby" or always flexible, I knew the Air Force to be unapologetically rigid. In this case, Joan, by virtue of being a physician, could not be my immediate supervisor. Working together was verboten.

Joan and I schemed to make the Air Force work for us. While my commitment was finished, Joan still owed four years. We pleaded with administration to allow me to take on Joan's commitment. Their answer, a swift and emphatic "no."

So I turned down my promotion to major, not even halfway to my goal of becoming a colonel. My meteoric rise had been cut short. The Air Force was losing an enthusiastic and willing participant at a time they could sorely afford to lose my experience and ability. Forced to leave my lifelong dream behind, I resigned with a sense of what I can only describe as grief—unwilling to live without my wife a moment longer—my metamorphosis into a devoted husband, and more importantly a good man, had become complete.

Or so I believed.

PART II

10

California Dreamin'

I began to fantasize about Joan's death shortly after we arrived in California. My fantasies came slithering effortlessly out of the abyss each time we had a disagreement, each time I allowed myself to think about how trapped I'd become. Travis Air Force Base in Fairfield, California boasted easy access to gourmet food, wine, and a plethora of outdoor and cultural activities. I was an avid bicyclist and had looked forward to riding the hills above the Napa Valley. Joan and I had eagerly anticipated skiing and boating at Lake Tahoe, as well as dressing formally for the symphony in San Francisco. All things considered, we'd hit the jackpot of assignments, and I should have felt extremely lucky.

Joan was one of three anesthesiologists with ten or so nurse anesthetists in a department run by a Lieutenant Colonel named Ken, a close friend of ours from Wilford Hall. Ken had created a civilian contract position for me in his department at Travis, the same job Joan and I had begged the Air Force personnel handlers to offer me. Not only was I hired to fill the exact same position, but I was offered a much higher salary, was not required to be on call, and had absolutely no chance of being deployed to a war zone—something I should have been ecstatic about.

Joan had rebounded from residency to become a well-respected anesthesiologist and teacher. We were sharing an office, teaching clinical anesthesia. Both voted clinical instructors of the year. We worked together, ate together, and even shared a ride to work most days. We'd finally found the stability we desired. At least Joan desired.

I, on the other hand, was missing my deployments.

This was for reasons far beyond the women I had once enjoyed. I missed the constant danger and dynamic way of living over my very stable/stagnant life in Northern California. My restlessness reached a peak when a young anesthetist I had taught—talented to be sure, maybe even as gifted as me, but with much less experience—was tasked to a Joint Special Operations group in Afghanistan. Just prior to leaving, he'd whined and moaned about not wanting to miss out on his lucrative moonlighting jobs in the civilian sector. I was sickened, not because I was above the love of money, but because I was jealous. One day he called me on a satellite phone from a mountain top while embedded with a team of special operatives. "Hey, bro, it's 'J.'" I don't know if I'm going to make it out of this hole. Promise me you'll take care of 'M' and 'L' for me." I quietly vowed that I would and silently, desperately wished I was in his place.

To counteract my boredom and to keep Joan in a manner in which she had become accustomed, I began covering OB anesthesia call at several nearby hospitals, figuring that if I couldn't attain military glory, I might as well become rich. I did become rich. At least my bank account—and my stock portfolio—grew exponentially. Within a few months, I was working every day of the week in one facility or another around the Bay Area. At St. Luke's in the Mission District of San Francisco, on the Delta at Sutter Delta, Kaiser Vallejo, and I was trying to fit UC Davis and Sutter Roseville into my schedule while continuing to work full time at the Air Force base. With my increased workload, my relationship with Joan began to unravel.

Subtle signs surfaced at first. For instance: Lying in bed exhausted one evening, Joan received a call from one of the nurse anesthetists we worked with. Joan was the on call anesthesiologist this night and available by phone. The surgeons were attempting to do something she felt wasn't safe. From an anesthesia point of view, surgeons were always walking the razor edge of patient safety to operate, especially in the middle of the night. We anesthesia providers made our money by keeping the patient alive while the surgeons tried—in our minds, anyway—to kill them. Joan was much more conservative than I. I also possessed several years of clinical experience over her, which did make a difference in our comfort level within the gray areas we so often worked. This night she remained, as always, steadfast in what she believed was right. She dug in her heels and told the anesthetist to delay the case and tune the patient up in the ICU prior to surgery the next day. Fifteen minutes later, she received a phone call from a blustery surgery resident. She told him in no uncertain terms that the case was not going to be done that night. Fifteen minutes later, the staff surgeon called. He was positively apoplectic. I could hear him from my side of the bed. Fifteen minutes after she refused him, the hospital commander, a general surgeon himself, called and tried to order her to do the case. While previously, when things were good with us, I would have stood up for her—I might have even taken the phone from her and talked with the surgeon—this night, I gave up and went to the guest bedroom to sleep, frustrated and irritated with her stubbornness. While Joan was technically well within the patient's best interest in her decision making, I wished she would have just done the case to get it over with and allow me to get back to sleep. One of the facets of her personality I'd loved most when we met was her determination and will to do the right thing. In my fatigue, I had come to loathe one of the most endearing parts of her personality.

Next, Joan wanted to buy a house. Our view on what we could afford couldn't have been more different. She had champagne tastes. Mine—more like beer—an outcome of having a father who had grown up rather poor and became a conservative banker. I had already emptied my entire life savings once to give Joan the wedding of her dreams—my duty, I felt as her fiancé—but I wasn't ready to empty joint accounts that I still thought of as mine for a supercilious purchase of a mansion when we would be just as comfortable in a standard three bedroom, two bath ranch style home not situated on a golf course.

"We can't afford it," I said as we sat awkwardly in the living room, surrounded by the sky blue carpet and stark white walls of our rental home as we talked about her list of acceptable homes—even though I knew we could.

"Sure we can. Someday I'll be out of the Air Force and can chip in."

"You don't get out for three more years. What about a down payment?"

"I've seen these things called ARMs. We could get one of those or a second mortgage."

One mortgage seemed overwhelming to me, let alone a second,

and I'd made sure that most of our money was tied up in retirement funds. Truth be told, Joan had no idea how much money we truly had.

"What if the market crashes?" I said.

"The interest rates are fantastic at around 6% right now. Five years ago, they were 18%."

She had obviously done her homework, and in the end, I felt powerless to say no. Taught by example by my father, I was allowed to have my own conservative opinions and beliefs, I just wasn't free to voice them to my wife or act on them. My job was to give her everything she wanted whether I thought it was a good idea or not. Deep down, I resented my compulsion/duty because I still felt antagonism between my parents' values and my own. Why was it okay for me to work three jobs while she planned to someday "chip in?" Our starter home was a $600,000 behemoth of a Northern California home.

And then Joan began pressuring me to begin a family. We were barely sleeping in the same bed, let alone making love. On most nights, one or the other of us would go to bed early and feign sleep as the other arrived. She believed a child of our own could fix our slowly weakening relationship. I couldn't begin to understand how a baby would solve our problems, but she became increasingly adamant. I was still very much interested in making money, saving money, traveling, and looking toward early retirement, but just for the two of us, and if completely honest, mostly for me. Having a baby to care for was the farthest thing from my mind.

But now that she wanted a child, Joan suddenly became very solicitous. And whether from a sense of duty or just pure desire, I gave in. We tried for six months with no luck, and the longer we were unsuccessful, the more obsessed Joan became, finally referring herself to a fertility specialist. So, we began monitoring her temperature and counting days. In the beginning, having sex regularly was a welcome change, but before long the act itself became a mere task to be completed, something without joy, especially when Joan began visiting one of my workplaces sixty miles from home urging me to "adjourn to my call room" on the appointed day at the prescribed hour.

My fantasies began simply—I didn't want a baby, but I had already given in to the idea. I quietly hoped one of us would be unable to reproduce. But as we continued trying, I realized I no longer wanted to be married. I contemplated divorce, but not as a realistic alternative. Divorce was 1) a sin, which had suddenly become important to me; and 2) the lazy person's way to address marital issues—lazier than sitting around waiting for my spouse to die. Joan was a Christian; she believed strongly that when she died, the next thing she would see was Christ in heaven. Seemed like a win-win situation. With Joan gone, I felt I would be free to reinvent myself and live on my terms, not hers.

Who knows how far these fantasies would have taken me, but around this time, Joan was asked to take a week off to travel to Montana to meet Loy, one of her classmates and a fellow member of her cherished women's group from medical school. She and Loy were going to the mountains to stay with Loy's friend, Christian, who owned a lodge on the border of the Bob Marshall Wilderness. I was relieved to have some time alone. Joan must have known I needed a break. I continued fantasizing about her death during her week away. In fact, the visions were much clearer. I knew she was flying. I imagined her plane falling out of the sky. I knew she'd be hiking in mountains. I imagined cliffs and rocky precipices.

In the midst of these fantasies, Joan returned. No more telltale worry lines at the corners of her eyes, no more pursed lips, and most of all, no more pushing to have a child. She seemed at peace.

She described her time with Loy at Christian's resort as spiritual. I was angry at first and thought, *Nice that she could go to a place on a lake in the mountains at a fancy resort with her best friend and a guy named Christian. I wonder how I can work out the same kind of trip with a girl named Kristina. Spiritual...* But as time went on, I could see her change was authentic, and I began to soften. I was curious but hesitant to believe her serenity would last. Over the next few weeks, though, without her obsessive pushing, I, too, began to feel more at ease, and we began making love—not at all to conceive a child, but simply because we wanted to.

When Joan became pregnant, something changed between us. The tranquility she'd gained and carried with her from the mountains of Montana was magnified. I opened up, too. We were suddenly able to communicate again—more easily and more deeply than we ever had. Anticipating a helpless infant, one who carried cells from both of us, awakened a deep sense of responsibility within me and finally forced me to consider something besides myself, something that was a part of me, but not me. Something that was totally dependent on us. Joan was perfectly capable of caring for herself, but our child needed us, me. This fact made me see Joan differently—with a softer eye. I silently committed to both of them.

Then came an unexpected gift. All civilian employees were released from their contracts at David Grant Medical Center. I was given a short week to vacate my office and return my keys. Though the loss of this job was a surprise, I was on great terms with the other civilian hospitals I had been working for, and within the week, I was the new chief of OB anesthesia at Sutter Delta Medical Center in Antioch, California.

My new schedule consisted of two twenty-four hour shifts a week which allowed me more time at home. My relationship with

Joan continued to flourish, and we spent valuable time in meaning-ful conversation, puttering around our home, spending time in the rose garden I'd planted, visiting people, and sometimes merely lying around reading. Joan became more fun, more carefree... or maybe the change was really in me as I recovered from working every day and many nights. Our togetherness was peaceful and unhurried, with-out the sense of desperation I had once felt. Joan was not busy at work which allowed her to be home much earlier in the day, and I was able to spend at least four days with her a week. We traveled through-out the Napa Valley, attended the orchestra and opera in San Fran-cisco. I cooked, which Joan dearly loved. So did I. Surprisingly to me, I also found Joan, in her second trimester, physically irresistible. She experienced no morning sickness—conversely she was feeling quite healthy. Her skin glowed, her checks were rosy, her breasts even fuller. I was absolutely fascinated by her body and couldn't get enough. Joan loved receiving the attention as much as I loved giving it, and as our physical bond matured, so did our emotional connection.

When the nightmares began, I discounted them. I assumed they were subconscious fears about having a baby or guilt about having previously wanted Joan dead. The dreams persisted, though, and be-came ever more frequent. I didn't tell her. Always similar. Joan and I are happily frolicking in the sun on some fabulous vacation in some faraway place. Riding elephants in Thailand, diving in Bali, climbing to Machu Pichu, but the happiness never lasts. The sunlight always fades to a dark and dreary twilight, and Joan's complexion becomes gray. Dark circles form under her eyes while I watch. The suppleness of her skin becomes paper thin, dry, and frail. I frantically call out for help. "I need to get her to a hospital! She's dying." Cancer. No one is around to hear. Only the trees and clouds darkening the sky.

11

October 22

I was sitting at the desk in the middle of the nurse's station at Sutter Delta Medical Center chatting amiably with the evening shift labor and delivery nurses when she called.

Halfway through my twenty-four-hour workday, my workload had slowed—at least for the time being. I was looking forward to retiring to my call room to watch a bit of television when the cell phone on my hip buzzed. I pulled it out of its holster, identified Joan's number, felt a pleasant sense of warmth and anticipation, expecting an update on her 25th week of pregnancy with a small discussion about how much she missed me in her soothing cara-mel-coated voice. I headed somewhere more private to chat and hadn't taken more than three steps when I felt—more than heard—her *hello*.

Halting and full of fear, her emotion was palpable. My entire world buckled.

Dropping into a nearby rolling chair, forcing myself to breathe, I blurted, "You have cancer, don't you?" And, "I'm on my way." Words seemed so inadequate. When I turned, five nurses stared intently at me with eyebrows furrowed and hands to faces or hearts. They'd been listening.

I didn't even try to maintain my usual strong façade. Tears rolled down my face. Standing to collect my bag, I barely registered the charge nurse making phone calls to cover the remainder of my shift.

I sprinted to my truck and drove with my pedal to the floor. It was 60 miles to David Grant Medical Center.

I have no recollection of being checked through the front gate of Travis Air Force Base, nor do I recall parking my truck. I don't remember my march to the door or through the long narrow hallway leading to the elevator. Every day for three years, I'd stridden to work down that very hallway and ridden that same elevator.

Now the ride to the fourth floor was agonizingly slow. I stood alone in the five-foot by five-foot box. My motorized carriage seemed a coffin. I focused on worst case scenarios, something I had been well-trained to do. My heart raced and my breath grew short as I watched the numbers for each floor appear.

On the fourth floor, the doors opened with a labored groan. I paused in front of the locked double doors of the L&D suite, needing one last moment before facing the physicians, the nurses I knew well, and most of all, Joan. I felt certain the moment I walked through, her life sentence would be pronounced.

I needed to be strong. The staff had seen me fight through many crises in those very rooms, and I believed they would expect the same in my own calamity. Feeling completely inadequate, I inhaled deeply, squared my shoulders, and walked with purpose to the intercom. Forced to beg admission to the locked obstetrical unit where I'd once worked, I fought to control my heart rate and slow my breathing, a trick I'd learned in dive school in Hawaii.

"In with the good, out with the bad. If you control your breathing, you control your heart rate. If you control your heart rate, you control your breathing. Everything stays in sync," my dive instructor had told me on the beach in Hawaii five years before.

I was alone, having been sent with a terribly ill patient from Osan Air Base, South Korea. The Air Force hospital where we'd been stationed in Korea had been dreadfully small. No ICU. No experienced nurses. Only newly minted ones with very little familiarity with such critically ill patients. Rob, the only general surgeon, and me, the only anesthetist, had been alone as far as experienced critical care providers, so we'd set up camp in the patient's room for forty-eight hours, around the clock. Eight hour shifts. One of us sleeping, one of us monitoring the patient. Even if we'd had experienced nurses, our hospital hadn't the capacity to care for this complicated case. So, we'd done the best we could with the few resources we had, then the two of us cared for him around the clock until we could arrange transport through the Air Force Air Evacuation system that I had once maligned with my personal hero, Steve, in flight nursing school.

After being awake for over ninety-six hours, the Air Evac powers that be had still preferred me awake, but obtunded, and in command of my patient for forty-eight more hours. In a plane full of empty litters, the nurse in charge had still refused to care for my patient and allow me to lie down. We finally landed in Hawaii, and I turned my patient over, but I remember nothing of my journey to billeting and subsequent walk to my room where I slept for a solid sixteen hours.

Upon waking, my first goal was to find food, then a dive master. I knew I was in for an indeterminate stay, and I had a few things on my agenda. I'd always wanted to get PADI certified, and I ended up being "stuck" on Oahu for over a month. Never one to let an opportunity pass, I took advantage of my time in limbo. While I waited, I dove. On return to Korea, my squadron commander attempted to bring me up on charges for misuse of government funds, but I'd been savvy enough to document my visit every morning to the Air Force transportation office and the fact I was told each morning there were no approved return flights. I hadn't really loved diving. While swimming through narrow lava tubes with no ambient light, my oxygen tanks banging on the ceiling, air hoses and regulator tangling in the outcroppings of the narrower and narrower tubes, I fought to control my growing sense of claustrophobia. My walk toward the nurse's station was much like that—attempting to control my panic as my vision became narrower and narrower. Fighting to appear calm. Sensing that if I lost control for even a millisecond, I would spiral out into the deep dark ocean, never to find my way back.

Joan's obstetrician stood just in front of the nurse's station in his usual khaki chinos and button down shirt—his full length white lab coat fell just below his knees. Alternately he rocked from toes to heels, his hands clasped behind his back. Though I could tell he was struggling to remain clinically distant, his eyes betrayed him with tension in the outer corners. Beside him was a woman, also in a long white lab coat, also obviously attempting to remain aloof. I registered her for a moment and wondered who she was. Jeff reached out and grasped my shoulder awkwardly.

He didn't waste time. "Joan has cancer, Darrin."

The woman reached out her hand as a greeting, and I now recognized that she'd been crying. Her eyes were red rimmed and tears still pooled slightly atop her lower lids. She introduced herself as Carolyn, a heme/onc physician. An old friend of Joan's.

"What kind?" I asked her.

"Looks like leukemia. I don't know yet if it's lymphocytic or my-elogenous."

Being no hematologist, the question was merely the reflex action of a seasoned medical provider. All I heard was "cancer." Joan had been given a death sentence. She and our unborn daughter were dying.

"Can I see her?"

"In a few minutes. We need to talk about treatment protocols."

"Can we do it with Joan?"

"We've already talked to her about them. She insisted."

I wasn't surprised. Joan would have wanted to spare me the shock of seeing her emotion.

Jeff explained the events of the day. Joan had been working when she became so disoriented that she nearly fainted and was forced to lie on the cold, hard, blood-spattered floor of an occupied operating room. Being a good (and stubborn) physician, she hadn't allowed anyone to assist her as she rose unsteadily to her feet, but gathered herself as quickly as she could and exited the room, walking imme-diately to the privacy of her office, the office I had so recently shared with her, where she performed an instant blood test on herself.

Throughout Joan's pregnancy, she had been weak, short of breath, and easily fatigued, but we had assured ourselves that her symptoms were run-of-the-mill pregnancy symptoms. Despite my regular nightmares, denial was a well-used tool in my life. Joan's too.

I imagined my grandfather, a self-made millionaire, sitting me down at his dark wood-colored Formica table in what passed for a breakfast area in their purely utilitarian conservative Dutch home. This was the second home my mother had lived in as a child, an upgrade, just down the block from the first, less modern home he and my grandmother had begun raising my mother and her five siblings in. Every Sunday afternoon for coffee and every holiday, my grandparents hosted huge, boisterous family gatherings where we kids had the entire basement to ourselves with its harvest gold and white pool table, ping-pong table, building blocks for the few boys, dolls for the many girls, and my favorite, the dark mechanical room, the even darker crawl space, and best of all, the very mysterious room without a light, behind the ping-pong table where I had once found a moonshine jug. I used to pretend this dark space was my secret lair.

This time, I was all alone across from my stony-faced grandfather with his widow's peak and aquiline nose. And I was intimidated. I'd been summoned because I'd chosen not to participate in Little League baseball that summer, and I was seated at his judgement table. I wondered if any of my cousins had been summoned in a similar way. Probably not. After all, I was the only one he had ever spanked, the only one who'd tried to beat up my aunt Carol.

He said, "Son."

I wasn't his son, and I could feel my face reddening with shame and finally anger.

"Vander Ploegs don't quit."

I wasn't quitting. I just wasn't going out.

"Are you a quitter?"

"No, Sir."

"Then why aren't you going out for baseball?"

"I don't like baseball."

"What does that have to do with anything?" he said with finality. "We've made a strong name for ourselves in this town. As a man, you have a duty to keep that name up."

Duty. My father felt just as strongly about duty. He served our family because of that duty. Duty and love were inexorably intertwined for us. I had seen it my entire life.

I reached Joan's room and paused just beyond her vision behind a door which was slightly ajar. She was adrift in her private world. In her defenselessness, she was more beautiful than I had seen her since our wedding day—but that day, she had been in her element, poised and confident. This night, with no one seemingly to witness, she looked weak and frightened, and her transparency moved me deeply. I felt I was seeing the real Joanie for the first time. I stood in no man's land, stuck for the moment, thinking of the wild swings Joan and I had experienced in our relationship, knowing that from that point forward, Joan, her illness, and our baby Alex would become my only focus.

I crossed the threshold.

I was all in.

Joan sat straighter in her bed, arranged her gown and the bedding. She met my eyes with her best level gaze. Her hair was perfectly combed, and her eyes, my favorite feature, usually so open and alive, immediately clouded to opaque screens. Foregoing emotion and comfort, we got down to the business of leukemia treatment. I distantly registered a sense of wistfulness, already missing the fleeting vulnerability I had witnessed a few short moments prior.

"They asked if we would consider aborting Alex."

"Let's worry about you right now. If Alex is harmed, we can have another baby once you're cured."

"What if she's born handicapped? What if my chemotherapy maims her or kills her?

"I can't control that right now. We'll still love her like nothing else."

"You'll need her someday."

"I need you now."

"You'll need her after I'm gone."

"I am here with you now, and you are here with me. I am grateful for that."

"Me too… I'm scared."

"I'll stay by your side, no matter what."

"I know you will. You're a good man, Darrin Dixon."

I thought, *I hope to God that is true.*

12

Admission

After spending a very restless night with me sharing her single hospital bed, Joan exited David Grant Medical Center on her way to the ambulance that would transfer her to U.C. Davis Medical Center and the definitive treatment for her leukemia. She was sitting awkwardly in a wheelchair with a stormy countenance. If the enormity of her new diagnosis hadn't completely overshadowed the levity of the situation, I'm afraid I would have laughed aloud. Joan's consternation had nothing to do with leukemia. She felt well (for the first time in several months), having been transfused with three units of packed red blood cells the evening before, the beginning of a constant stream of blood products pumped through her body to keep her failing system from shutting down.

A normal amount of blood coursing through her veins carrying vital nutrients to her organs agreed with her, but feeling stronger exposed her stubborn, ornery side.

"This sucks." She hung her head to hide her face from coworkers and patients.

"What sucks?" I was behind pushing her wheelchair. Jeff and Carolyn were on either side and slightly behind. She couldn't see my grin or the faces I made to her physicians.

"I'm a doctor, for goodness sake. Why can't they just let me walk out of here?"

"Even David Grant's favorite daughter has to follow the rules sometimes, Princess."

I was struggling to maintain my composure at Joan's frustration at being a patient. I remained behind her—thankfully hidden from view.

"I'm getting out of this chair."

Gently resting my hand on her shoulder I attempted to dissuade her, as my other hand continued to guide her wheelchair.

Her head suddenly straightened along with her posture as she spied the ambulance. She couldn't imagine being turned over to the paramedics as anything more than a proud patient/physician who would not go gently into that dark night. She was glorious in her stubbornness.

The fact that Joan's physicians accompanied us on our journey to the ambulance was both endearing and slightly unnerving. Our casual lighthearted stroll was the beginning of Joan's journey as a patient and my journey toward becoming the doting husband of the amazing pregnant lady doctor down the hall who happened to have cancer.

Watching her ambulance pull into the street, struggling in vain to spy her through the tinted glass, I imagined Joan's face pressed forlornly to the window, a small child tearfully riding away with grandpa and grandma for the first time—parents slowly fading into the distance.

I had never been to this part of U.C. Davis Medical Center. After her sixty-mile journey, Joan's ambulance turned to the left to enter the emergency bay where she would be unloaded. I was forced to the right. Parking lot after parking lot, all completely full. My impatience and fear rose with each successive, tightly packed lot. The sheer enormity of the looming towers and squat unwelcoming buildings that made up the medical center added to my growing discomfort. Searching frantically through each successive lot for a place to park, I became more upset. Finally, my last chance, a multiple story parking garage, but as I wound my way up the ramp, my anguish became volcanic. I physically felt Joan's fear across the vast acres of packed lots as I imagined her beginning the process of being admitted, to remain quite possibly for the rest of her life. She was alone and terrified. I was stuck trying to find a place to park my fucking truck!

By the time I'd parked at the very top of the garage, Joan had been admitted directly to the hematology/oncology unit, bypassing the emergency department, due to her already fragile immune system. I sprinted directly to the bank of elevators. Struggling to remain under control, I felt utterly transparent. I sensed first surprise, then pity from the occupants of the elevator as I huddled, close to the corner, out of breath, in my rumpled, tear-stained clothes that I'd been wearing now for more than two days—fear oozing from every pore.

On the heme/onc floor, the cheery décor of the first floor changed, the mood darkened. The area surrounding the elevator remained as bright, but the unit I walked toward bore kitschy pictures in heavy frames on its long hallway walls. Far from the excitement and miracles of labor and delivery, where I spent most of my time, cancer wards were frequently grim, forgotten. The new wood panel-ing near the elevator transitioned abruptly to dingy beige wallpaper. The floor was covered with some sort of vinyl manufactured—but not quite able—to look like porcelain tile. Overhead were long in-dustrial neon lights, the greenish light washing out shadows, casting a harsh cheap pall over the long walkway. To add to the lifeless at-mosphere, a locked door and an intercom greeted me, the spouse of a cancer patient, just as it had at the threshold of David Grant's OB ward. My feeling of transparency persisted as I strode past the nurses and physicians deeply immersed in their daily routines. The unit was full, and I registered for the first time that we weren't alone. In fact, we were surrounded with people afflicted by cancer in various stages of treatment—some fared better, many much worse. I paused at the nurse's station to introduce myself.

Joan's nurse offered to escort me. My sense of gloom heightened as we arrived in front of what looked like a huge vault door.

She knocked for me.

Joan sat placidly with legs crossed, wearing a light green hospital gown. Her auburn hair and reddish highlights shone in the midday light. She had recently adopted a shoulder length style, having cut her waist length hair for the first time since we had met in San Anto-nio. Her new "do" perfectly framed her face and hinted at her subtle sassiness. I loved it, and she was well aware of my fondness.

We didn't waste time, but immediately got down to making Joan's room our home by arranging the furniture to allow her the best view of her windows. We browsed through the bedside table, explored the bathroom, and placed our few personal items within easy access. Meanwhile, various hospital employees knocked and entered to complete tasks required for admission.

Then a more assertive knock sounded, and a young man entered without waiting for our reply. His hair was reddish brown and he wore a well-trimmed goatee, presumably his attempt at appearing older than he was. Dressed in a dark red plaid shirt, khaki pants, a worn brown belt, loafers, and the long white coat of a staff physician he introduced himself. "I'm Dr. G., the heme/onc fellow." Indignation suddenly boiled up from deep inside me. Why would they send a fellow to treat a staff physician? Despite my misgivings, Dr. G. quickly demonstrated his grasp of Joan's condition and proved he was an expert, the one actually treating patients in the rooms as opposed to staff like me who sat in their office drinking coffee and shooting the breeze while "teaching."

Next, Joan underwent an ultrasound. The obstetrics staff introduced themselves—along with the high risk obstetrician/perinatologist—who would be following her while she received her cancer treatment. The ultrasound and biophysical profile, a measurement of Alex's wellbeing, were promising in their initial assessment. They would be used as a baseline to measure her growth in utero hence forth and to assess the amount of amniotic fluid surrounding her. The bevy of obstetrics personnel found nothing worrisome in the ultrasound, aside from Alex being quite small for gestational age and considered "skinny" due to lack of nourishment secondary to Joan's condition.

Meeting the OB team and Joan's new perinatologist went a long way toward allaying our initial fears. The night before, Carolyn had told us that Joan would be dead within two to three weeks if she didn't undergo treatment immediately. Dr. G. had agreed. The night before, when we had hesitantly inquired how Joan's chemotherapy would affect Alex, we were told basically, "We don't know." Not enough research existed. We'd been given the option to deliver Alex by emergency cesarean section to avoid exposure to Joan's chemotherapy. At 25 weeks gestation, Alex was barely considered viable. If she survived, she would likely suffer severe lung damage, eye damage, brain damage, and/or digestive system damage to name a few of the dangers. The option to deliver her immediately also left Joan in danger. Her blood counts, oxygen carrying capacity, and ability to form clots to control her own bleeding from surgery were already severely compromised. We had also been given a second option, to terminate Joan's pregnancy to avoid poisoning Alex and allow Joan to undergo her treatment without a fetus's health to consider.

But now we had a third: throw caution to the wind and forge ahead. The fact that Alex would be monitored every day for signs of distress provided us with more reassurance and made us even more relieved to have chosen not to abort our baby or undergo a very risky cesarean section. All in all, we felt relatively hopeful about choosing treatment.

For Joan, her decision was based on a belief that God would watch over both of them. For me, the idea of trusting God to cure them seemed like a good idea, but I felt more comfortable choosing to trust the doctors we had just met and holding out hope that maybe God would help them.

Too soon after the ultrasound, Dr. G. returned with his young resident physicians in-tow. He asked if we would allow them to observe the first of Joan's many bone marrow biopsies. Joan and I had both taught residents and believed in education but were unsettled in our new role as guinea pigs. We did eventually consent, but I resolved privately to forcibly remove each from the room at the slightest comment or wayward glance.

Dr. G. removed a syringe from his pocket. That got my attention. Syringes were something I used every day.

He gently, almost sheepishly, explained to Joan that he was about to sedate her for the coming procedure. He looked genuinely surprised, eyebrows up, face beginning to flush as Joan crossed her arms, shook her head, and said, "No," in a manner which left no room for negotiation. Barbiturates (sedatives) have been known to cause birth defects in fetuses. Joan refused to accept that possibility for her child. In truth, in the third trimester of pregnancy, sedatives have little to no effect on fetuses unless used habitually by the mother. She knew this very well. But knowing that in theory meant nothing. She insisted on having the biopsy performed without sedation, and I felt I had no choice but to allow her that control. Dr. G. finally acquiesced. He was nervous, and the telltale signs began to appear as he requested in his quiet voice that she lie on her left side curled in a fetal position. Much more easily said than done for a pregnant woman.

His eyes were liquid and alive, sad as he twisted the long needle onto the syringe and withdrew the local anesthetic from a glass vial. I knelt to the right side of Joan's bed with my face gently against her's—whispering important things and stupid things, anything to distract her from the excruciatingly painful procedure she was about to endure. I brushed my fingers through her hair, a gesture she loved, knowing I would be unable to soothe her in that way in the near future—she would soon lose her hair. What was she thinking? Had she gone to her "happy place?" I imagined her running with Minnie, Mickey, and all the Disney characters she adored. I hoped she was there. I prayed she would be oblivious to the coming pain.

A barely audible moan escaped her lips as the needle bit sharply into her flesh and the local anesthetic infiltrated her tissues. Dr. G. injected more anesthetic that day than I had ever seen any physician inject for the procedure he was about to perform. Involuntarily calculating the toxic dosage in my head, something I did daily in the operating room, I realized he exceeded the technical threshold for a drug whose side effects included seizures and cardiovascular collapse. But I quietly thanked him, knowing the medication would not be absorbed in large amounts from her relatively less vascular hip and was therefore of little factor. He was being kind, and while some would have called him cavalier, I understood immediately that he practiced with common sense as well as "cookbook" theory to treat his patients—ironically in direct contrast to the way Joan sometimes practiced. I recalled the night in bed and Joan's staunch refusal to do a case she thought was too dangerous, then was brought back to the present by what Dr. G. did next.

He withdrew the aspirating needle and introducer from the package, and I recoiled. While I had anesthetized many patients for bone marrow biopsies, I had no recollection of the appearance of the needle—actually a large screw. I had become somewhat immune to the feeling of inserting large needles into my patients each day, but anticipating something this large being screwed into the hip of the person I loved most in the world without sedation sent chills down my spine.

Dr. G. quickly and skillfully incised Joan's right hip. The gaping hole was essentially bloodless due to the epinephrine in the local anesthetic acting to constrict her vessels. The deep red fluid that did escape was rapidly removed with gauze sponges. Joan didn't feel the knife entering her body.

I watched him hesitate, close his eyes, and inhale deeply as he said, "Okay, we're going to start now, and it's going to hurt."

Joan said, "Okay," in her small, timid voice and grunted almost imperceptibly as Dr. G. slowly rotated the screw more and more firmly until he was finally standing on the tips of his toes. Mercifully, his body fell slightly forward and downward as the tip of his needle entered the inner cavity of Joan's hip. He unscrewed the cap from the aspirating needle and twisted a thirty milliliter syringe to the hub and pulled back forcefully on the plunger, aspirating a deep red, almost gelatinous substance, a substance some felt a human's soul resided in, the very essence of Joan's being.

As a resident opened the specimen bottles, Dr. G. pushed the concoction of cells out of the syringe.

In each vial, the shape of the cigars I loved to smoke each time I visited Honduras, lay our entire future. Crystal balls. Only the bottles knew if we would be a family of three, intact and healthy or handicapped, or two, a daddy and little girl, or even just one.

[13]

Game Face

I'd dealt with a cancer diagnosis previously. That time it was my dad. We were summoned for a family meeting, which was out of the ordinary. Dad was pale and thinner than I'd ever seen him. We'd known something was wrong, but no one had dared ask. We didn't talk about things like that. I was a first year nursing student with a psych minor, and I'd attempted every new trick I'd learned to get him to tell us what he was going through. He didn't. Next thing I knew, he was in the hospital, and we were told he might not make it five years—a pronouncement that to me, as a barely more than teenage boy, was as frightening as Joan's diagnosis. But my dad had made it through his battle. He was a giant, invincible, with just enough mean in him to beat his cancer. I was already sure Joan wouldn't. She was much too tenderhearted and kind.

———

While awaiting Joan's bone marrow biopsy results, I called my parents. I told them their daughter-in-law—whom they loved as much as their own two daughters—had been diagnosed with cancer and their first female grandchild was in grave danger. I didn't sugarcoat the news. They deserved it straight, but I wondered how we would deal as a family with what could be prolonged treatment.

Joan's mother was more difficult. I had no history with Sandra. I didn't know how she would react to bad news. I only knew her from what little Joan had told me. Her description didn't lend me any confidence. Joan had always felt like her mom's mom. I held my own judgements about how she would handle Joan's diagnosis, and I was at a loss as to the best way to break the news. I could have left it for Joan to do. I wanted her to do it. Even more, I wanted anyone but me to deliver that bad news, but I felt it my duty to protect Joan. And as unpleasant as the task was, I went about my role seriously.

The phone rang three times. She answered. I simply said, "Sandra, Joan has cancer. We're at U.C. Davis Medical Center just across town from you."

"Oh, okay," was all she came up with.

"I'll call you back when we are able to have visitors."

I was flabbergasted. I couldn't understand her response, or more likely, her lack of response. Luckily, one of us hung up the phone, for the more I thought about it, the angrier I became.

We were actually able to have visitors at that point, but I hadn't told her. Joan and I needed time to settle in. I needed time to sort things out in my head. At the moment, there was so much internal noise that I could barely keep it together for Joan. I didn't need Sandra to add to our distractions.

———

I'd like to say we sat for hours immersed in meaningful conversations, but we didn't. We occupied ourselves in any way we could, playing board games, listening to music, and even singing, but the time still passed with agonizing slowness. We felt like laboratory rats locked in our twelve-by-twelve quarantined cage.

The all-important results came the next day. We sensed this by the quality of the knock. Dr. G. walked furtively into the room, his entourage in tow. He wasn't his light and airy self. Instead, he wore a frown and wouldn't meet our eyes. While I appreciated seeing his real concern, I bet that he wouldn't last long in his chosen field with that type of emotional output.

He peered down at us with a furrowed brow and then focused on the chart he held in his hands. Words seemed to stick in his mouth for just a moment before he collected himself. "The results of your bone marrow biopsy are back."

Joan sat stone faced, though I could see telltale signs of distress around her eyes.

Blood rushed furiously past my eardrums. Whoosh whoosh.

Knowing her diagnosis would enable us to move forward with treatment instead of living in perpetual limbo, we nodded to urge him on. Only a few days had passed, but waiting for "the word" was killing us—quite literally in Joan's case.

Dr. G. said a lot of words in the speech he had obviously prepared, and we both sat very still as if listening.

"Blah, blah, blah."

That's what I heard. Maybe Joan was doing a better job of interpreting. The only thing I really understood was "You have leukemia—what we call acute biphenotypic leukemia."

Neither Joan nor I said a word. Did she already know something

I did not? I had never heard of biphenotypic leukemia. Had she learned about it in medical school?

"Biphenotypic leukemia is the most difficult type of acute leukemia to treat," Dr. G. said before leaving us alone.

Neither of us moved a muscle, nor showed any emotion. We weren't accustomed to displaying any reaction at all. Anesthesia is all about aesthetics—if you look scared, you are scared; if you look calm, you are calm—we are only as good as we look. Joan had finally become butter-smooth like me with her "anesthesia face."

[14]

The Angry One

Neither Joan nor I could predict what would happen with her first treatment. We were acquainted with the medication names and the sequence in which they would be given. We even knew how many days the treatment would last, but we didn't know how the onerous side-effects would manifest themselves.

While beginning treatment was a significant milestone, we expected more—more than, well, nothing. Each day a nurse came in and wrote the cocktail du jour and schedule of administration on the treatment calendar. That simple piece of paper was the one thing we were able to use to concretely gauge Joan's progress—a day-to-day diary of our life.

The nurse whose job it was to administer the chemo wore a mask and gloves as she handled the little bag of fluid. The contents were a yellowish color, turning, twisting, and waving little tendrils as the medicine slowly mixed with its clear carrier solution and began to creep down the hollow tube. The IV bag was covered with foil, adding to its sinister feel. In the gravity of the moment, I "saw" something from a bad horror film—the fluid glowing, and the nurse wearing a hazmat suit. I had experience with hazmat suits.

Stuck. More like imprisoned on a decommissioned National Guard base somewhere in the vicinity of Denver, Colorado. I was part of a surgical team deployed in case of a terrorist attack on the Big Eight Summit. Caught in a maelstrom, wind whipping so ferociously that I couldn't hear what the guy next to me was yelling, we wore hazmat suits which also acted as a sort of sail in the high wind as we struggled to remain in position. Someone had escaped from the hot zone, using the tempest as cover, but had in time been recovered by our security team—a bunch of U.S. Marines from a unit called CBRF (Chemical Biological Response Force). The escapee had mysteriously suffered a separated sterno-clavicular joint and unknown other injuries, courtesy of one of the four hundred other Marines with whom I was deployed. We didn't know yet if he required surgery. What a night. The scenario was just a drill. The injuries were real. The escapee was a Marine, too. Playing a part. His buddies beat him unconscious because that's what they were trained to do. We put him back together.

It was that kind of training that kept me moving forward through the process of Joan's treatment. Just doing the next right thing. Not thinking too far ahead.

We held our breath as the IV fluid slowly dripped, the toxic elixir slowly flowing. Eventually reaching her arm and disappearing through her IV catheter.

"I'm not throwing up yet," Joan joked to break the overwhelming tension.

"Nope. Do you feel sick?"

"No. Is my hair falling out?" She had ornery little crinkles in the corners of her eyes.

"No."

"Phew!"

Joan was forced to undergo bone marrow biopsy after bone marrow biopsy, refusing sedation with each. I felt like the star in the movie "Groundhog Day" each time I begged her, "Will you please let them give you some fentanyl? At least versed?"

"No, I'll be okay. I don't want to take any chances with Alex."

Time after time, I found myself kneeling at her bedside, holding her hand and stroking her hair.

I could sense she was frightened, but Joan gritted her teeth, pursed her lips, and tightly clenched her eyes. In through her nose and out through her mouth the air came and went as she tried to blow her pain away. Her attempts weren't effective. Watching her suffer needlessly didn't ever become easier—but Joan was adamant about exposing our child to as few drugs as possible. Even if the chance the medication would affect our baby was miniscule, Joan chose to control the one thing she could—and this one thing wore on me as she dragged me right along with her through her torture.

For all Joan's strength and mine, the hospital was challenging us in different ways. As Joan's treatment continued and the monitoring of her pregnancy became more intense, I found myself unable to refer to the baby by name.

"How's the baby today?" I always asked after each ultrasound.

One day, Joan said, "Don't you like her name? You helped pick it."

"I love her name," I said. But the truth was, I had become so overwhelmed by Joan's condition, I was unable to fully give myself over to Alex. Although Alex remained small for gestational age, her head remained stubbornly on the growth curve, she remained active, surrounded by adequate amniotic fluid, and we were able to see her breathe—a sign she was faring okay. And yet, no matter how many times I heard her, felt her kick, and saw her on a screen, I remained aloof, shielding myself from the possibility that she might die.

"Alex is going to be alright. I don't know how to explain it. I just know."

"Did God tell you?" I said without restraining my sarcasm.

"Speaking of names," Joan continued, "no one calls me by my own name anymore." Her words were true. Most of the staff just came in and said, "Hey." "The nurses barely even acknowledge my presence. Especially the night nurses. I feel like they come in, take my vitals, give me my treatments, post my numbers on the treatment calendar, and leave. I know it's a cliché, but I feel like a disease."

I was thinking, *You feel like a disease? You are the center of attention. I'm just the husband of the pregnant woman with leukemia. You're famous. I'm invisible.* But I said nothing.

Our life consisted of tests, numbers, and isolation—isolation because Joan's immune system was being decimated by the drugs—on purpose—something I never could get my mind around. No one came to visit—they couldn't have anyway. Though I'd finally put the word of her condition out, Joan wasn't allowed visitors anymore except immediate family. On the fourth or fifth day of her hospitalization, even I was forced to leave after coming down with a common cold that was literally a mortal threat to her. The nurses unceremoniously removed me from her room and the entire heme/onc unit after hearing the beginnings of a cough. They were acutely tuned in to signs and symptoms of systemic infections. I left with a sense of sadness, but also secretly a little relief, with an excuse to spend a couple of days in our lovely, quiet, private home—the home I had once been reticent to buy.

Because no one could visit, everyone clamored for information. I was doing my best to put out regular email updates and calls to my parents, who then distributed the information to various groups of people, but my heart was not in it. The urge to pray had been hardwired into me, so I kept my updates spiritual, but the only reason I communicated at all was my ever present sense of duty as husband to Joan.

My updates did have one nice outcome for Joan. Get well cards began to arrive from around the globe. We were inundated with little notes of prayers and reports of prayers. And yet, I derived no comfort from them for myself. Though I believed in God's ability to cure Joan, I felt no sense that He would. I found myself once again on the terribly uncomfortable wooden bench doing my best to pay attention while the lady harangued me, ironically, with examples of our supposedly loving, benevolent God. The huge pages were thrown back over her easel as she told story after story of Jesus healing the sick, of God protecting those who loved Him, those who chose Him, of people asking for miracles and receiving them. I believed the stories then. I was trying to now, but I found myself metaphorically sitting at the feet of the other God I had been introduced to as a child. The angry One. I imagined being witness to a vengeful God as he smote Joan because of my lack of faith, or because I had committed one too many sins.

News of Joan's faith, however, soon travelled around the hospital. All types of nurses and physicians began knocking on our door. They all asked one thing. "How do you do it? How can you remain so positive—accept your illness in light of its likely outcome?" The visitors all knew Joan was a physician and I was a nurse anesthetist, and despite the party line of sunshine and roses we were being given by most, they assumed we knew better.

One afternoon, sitting by the big windows, looking out across the Sacramento skyline, I asked Joan, "Are you acting, or are you really that sure that God will take care of you and Alex?"

"God will take care of us. He always has."

She said the words as if there was no doubt.

I felt pretty pathetic. "I've never thought of it like that. I believe with all my heart that God *can* take care of all of us. My problem is I don't know if he *will*."

"You're going to be okay, Darrin. God told me."

"God told you?"

She nodded.

"Why doesn't he tell me?

"Have you asked?"

No, I had not asked, but after that, I began waking around five o'clock in the morning before Joan awoke so I could sit and watch her. I had always loved watching her sleep—the only time she appeared truly peaceful—her lips pursed in a way uniquely hers, eyelids softly closed, telltale tension absent from her face as she quietly murmured and lulled me into a trance. In those moments, I was sometimes able to pray.

[15]

My Surrender

Having felt the slightest hint of God, I returned to work.

My first night back at Sutter Delta after two weeks with Joan, as I lay in my call room, again almost halfway through my shift, sixty miles away from Joan in her hospital bed, I received a call from her nurse. All her nurses had become dear to us, but this one was special—compassionate and positive while remaining honest and to the point. Just the way we liked our news. Seeing the U.C. Davis prefix on the screen of my phone instantly brought about a reaction that was undoubtedly out of proportion to what it should have been, but by then my nerves were frayed to the point of breaking. Everything seemed life threatening at that moment.

"Is she dead?" I asked in all seriousness.

"No, but she's in the ICU. You should come. She doesn't look good. We had to code her."

———

I conjured the macabre scene: two nurses running down a hallway pushing the bed, a pale lifeless body, sheets askew, a monitor
screeching. A third nurse on her knees straddling the lifeless body,
pushing medications through her IV with one hand while forcing air
into her lungs via a breathing bag with the other. A scenario I had
seen play out more times than I cared in real life. The only difference… this patient was my wife.

In a bit of déjà vu, I scrambled to get someone to cover my shift
and rushed to Sacramento. I curled up in the ICU waiting room,
terrified for Joan, but even more terrified for Alex. Faced with her
possible death, for the first time I became as protective of Alex as I
was of Joan. When a human body shuts down like Joan's had, it pref-
erentially shunts blood and oxygen to its most vital organs, foremost
the brain and heart. The body doesn't consider a baby to be vital.
The placenta is one of the first organs to have blood diverted from it
because a baby is seen as somewhat of a parasite. No one could tell
me how long Alex had been without oxygen, but the likelihood was
that she had been hypoxic for some period of time.

By noon the next day, Joan emerged through the swinging double
doors of the ICU looking only slightly worn from her ordeal. She
was sporting several bruises and a bandage on her wrist—signs of
attempts by someone to insert an arterial line to monitor her then
non-existent blood pressure. She also wore a bandage over her right
breast where her old infected catheter, the source of her sepsis, had
been located.

I flashed back to our first meeting in the anesthesia call room at

Wilford Hall—the day I fell in love with her. The day my life changed for good. I was as bashful as a teenage boy with his first real crush. I'd done my best not to get caught ogling her breast as I tried to see her nametag that day. This day, I chuckled. We were so far past that now.

A new large IV had sprouted from her neck overnight with three separate lines protruding from the surface of her skin—reminders of what she had endured in my absence. She was also totally bald—undoubtedly the most beautiful bald women I had ever seen, but her lack of hair was shocking.

Later, her brush with death already forgotten, she began internet shopping for the perfect wig with the correct style and color to suit her. I wasn't crazy about the wig she found. She'd picked it because of its similarity to her own hair, but it came up miles short. The color was close, the style identical, but it lacked the essence of her natural hair. There were no shimmering red highlights, no hairs slightly askew. It looked... well, lifeless. Yet, she felt less conspicuous with it on, and that was the important thing. She also loved hats and now requested and wore the many gifted hats she received as her mood dictated, but never over her wig. It was either/or.

Still stuck in her prison of a room, we searched for things to talk about.

"Did you get those guys to help you roof the shed?" she asked one day as we sat halfheartedly playing Scrabble.

"No, I just did it myself. It actually looks pretty good. Guess I have another line of work if this anesthesia thing doesn't pan out."

"You're good at whatever you want to be good at."

"You're kind."

Again our life went from what seemed like hell to something resembling mundane. We arose each morning; I stayed with Joan most nights. We showered, made the bed, did her vital signs, got blood drawn, did biophysical profiles, received chemotherapy, got x-rays, read letters that we'd received, talked with the various staff that continued to visit, read, played Scrabble, listened to Christian and classical music, took naps, did crossword puzzles, and attempted to make life as bearable for each other as we could. I also worked some during that time—once in a while when Joan's mom was able to stay with her. I even went home to make sure the house was still standing—with the added benefit of being able to sleep in my own bed.

One night, I sat alone at my home computer considering our lives—the future, the present, and the past we would never get back. We were faced with too many unknowns. I was afraid for Joan. I was afraid for Alex. I was afraid for myself. But my fear wasn't terror. It was worse. All I could see at that moment was a very long and exhausting road leading to two equally unpalatable outcomes. One in which I was totally alone after the loss of my wife and daughter. Or one in which I still shared my life with Joan and Alex, but with one or both of them permanently disabled to an as-yet-unknown degree. I was exhausted and becoming hopeless and couldn't yet grasp a future in which we were all healthy. I attempted to write an update for our family and friends—nothing came. My fingers wouldn't move, as if my brain and digits weren't connected by their finely interwoven plexuses of nerves. Finally, allowing my mind to wander, letting the quiet wash over me, my fingers began to type what was really in my heart. Though I had only the one experience as a twelve-year-old with such a phenomenon, I felt very strongly that the spirit of God came to me as I accepted His words. I finally found my elusive full surrender:

My Surrender

I kneel before You today a broken man.
Last week, I stood tall and proud in front of You, certain You knew
    how great an asset I was.
This week, I know I am only what You make me.
The gifts that I have are just that—gifts You have given me.
Yesterday, I was an important man.
Today, I am nothing—knowing every breath I am allowed to take is
    a gift from You.
One hour ago, I spoke loudly about what I thought would be best for US.
Now I raise my head from the floor and—in a whisper—ask what You
    would have me do.
Ten minutes ago, my aim was to make my life a dream.
I know now my only purpose is to glorify Your name.
Three and a half weeks ago, I didn't know if my wife and unborn child
    would live to see Thanksgiving.
Today, You have given us hope for the future and something to be truly
    thankful for.
In the blink of an eye, You took everything from me, stripped me of
    all I hold dear.
You forced me to the floor and wouldn't let me stand.
Just when I thought I couldn't go on, You showed me the way.
You picked me up and breathed into me Your breath of life.
You showed me a new way of living, free of the illusion of control.
You showed me to trust You and You alone.
You told me that if I sincerely asked for Your help, You would always
    be there.
When I forget to breathe, You will breathe for me.
When I can't find my way, You will guide me.
Today I kneel before You with only one purpose,
To begin repaying my debt,
Knowing that without You, I am nothing…

16

The Rabi

About that time, our pastor from Napa Seventh Day Adventist Church came to visit. Curious timing after experiencing my own personal God moment and "surrender." I'd never spoken to him personally. In truth, I was only going to church every Sabbath for three reasons. The most important was that Joan wanted me to. The second was that, with my upbringing, church was just something we had to do as a couple. The third reason was purely selfish. Attending the Napa church always meant we could eat lunch at a fantastic restaurant or picnic at one of the many wineries. Wine was biblical after all, despite the cries of our conservative religion that the wine Jesus and his disciples drank at the Last Supper was not fermented. I didn't attend because I felt I would get anything out of the service. I certainly didn't go to do what I knew I was supposed to do—worship and praise God.

Joan was my own personal twenty-four hour a day example of how to live with faith, how to have a personal relationship with God, how to love, but it wasn't enough. Though I'd had two separate deeply personal impressions of Him, I had still never heard God speak as Joan had. I'd never felt His loving arms around me like she did, and I was jealous. Joan, from what she said, grew up living and breathing God and Jesus. I believed her, but I viewed these things as an unfair advantage. I needed more.

Joan already exhibited an otherworldly sense of serenity about her plight. She carried on through her days as if she had a comforter perched on her shoulder soothing her, giving her secret words that allowed her to remain above the fray. I spent the majority of each day attempting to hide my anger and confusion, busying myself with the mundane to avoid my deeper feelings. I desperately desired what she had, whether it was my childhood God or an altogether different God. When the nurses called to tell us someone was here to see us, and I walked out to greet our mystery guest and found Pastor Wray, I wondered what to do. I wasn't sure I wanted a preacher to intrude with the typical *rah rah Jesus and faith* speech. I was already sick to death of that.

Pastor Wray was of average height and weight. The hair on top of his head had long ago disappeared, though he didn't seem quite old enough to be bald. The hair on the sides of his head was short, but still long enough to be mussed from the motorcycle helmet he carried in his left hand. He wore jeans, black riding boots, and a worn black leather jacket. He apparently hadn't lied when he'd called himself a "motorcycle riding pastor." I knew he'd only come to believe in Christ as an adult and that he was also somewhat of a renegade—a pastor who accomplished the mission of Christ like I accomplished the mission of the Air Force, in an unconventional way. He was also an outspoken critic of the religious establishment and gave voice to many of the issues that floated around in my head—like the silliness of arguing the minutiae of the Bible and the futileness of trying to make one's diet a matter of salvation—when it all came down to interpretation. After all, none of us was there when it was written. I identified strongly with him, but I still wasn't sure I was ready for the visit. As I contemplated how our first meeting would play out, I recalled a story of how my dad kicked our hometown pastor out of our home when I was very young. I was prepared to do the same from our hospital room. I took my job as gatekeeper seriously.

"Hello, my friend. Seems like you and Joan have had a rough go of it."

He said this in a husky voice—as if he had sustained vocal cord damage of some type. I laughed to myself. Only an anesthesia provider would think of vocal cord damage instead of something simpler—a strain from overuse—this would be a vocational hazard of preaching the gospel and visiting with people every day.

Joan and I had never been active in his church in the traditional sense. We didn't keep in contact with anyone outside of Saturday morning worship. We mostly attended, sat in the back, sang the songs, listened to special music, then the sermon, and quietly left before anyone had a chance to ask us to lunch at their home, keeping us from one of our favorite restaurants. I was surprised he even knew who we were. He certainly didn't know me well enough to call me friend, yet I felt I owed him about ten seconds, since he had made the forty-five-minute trip in the middle of the week just to see us.

"Yeah, we've had a bit of a challenge."

"How's Joan?" At least he didn't call her JoAnn as so many were prone to do.

"She's doing okay."

He didn't ask if he could see her. My body language was loud and clear. He was obviously perceptive. He didn't push. I grudgingly gave him a point for that.

"So, how are you doing? It seems like it might be harder to watch someone you love go through all this pain than to actually go through it yourself."

That was the first time I had heard someone say something like that. He'd just put words to feelings that had been lurking deep within me, but that I couldn't say out loud for fear of seeming selfish.

"I'm doing better than her. She's dying," I said roughly, not yet willing to confide my hidden feelings.

He didn't bat an eye. "Do you want to go grab some coffee?

Coffee. I had gone round and round with any Adventist I could corner about coffee. Supposedly Ellen G. White, who incidentally had lived in the Napa Valley—in her visions—determined that God, the source of her visions, considered coffee off limits. In my opinion, devout Adventists had turned her "health message" into a sort of salvation by diet edict. I was having a very difficult time understanding visions about a healthy diet sent from God, visions from God at all really. I especially had a problem with three of the forbidden types of food—meat, something near to my heart. The other two were coffee and wine, both of which I'd cultivated a highly developed taste for. I loved everything about them—from their origins and the way the beans and grapes were grown to the type of grind, time under steam pressure, and finally the cupping of the coffee and the very similar way in which wine was created, decanted, poured, and drunk.

But, here was an Adventist pastor suggesting that we go drink coffee. Maybe I was starving for friendship, maybe I couldn't even admit that to myself, maybe I was completely unable to show my feelings to Joan, but I sensed my confidante had just arrived on his motorized steed.

I told the nurse we were leaving for a while, then we walked down the hall, down the elevator, out the door, and across the street to a little coffee shop to get fresh air, coffee, and probably even a pastry.

The décor was somewhat upscale, sort of wine country chic with lots of earth tones brushed on stucco and bare metal beams on the ceiling. It was bustling as usual with some business looking types and many more medical people in various colored scrubs, some with paper OR hats, masks, and shoe covers tucked into their pockets. We sat down at a corner table after getting our coffee.

He didn't mince words. "So how ya feeling about God these days?"

"Umm, conflicted."

"I can only imagine. What's your background?"

"I'm a Baptist. Have been my entire life. Church three times a week whether I needed it or not…"

More visions of church as a child assaulted me. This time, I was sitting in the back pew with three of my friends. Hungover. I was only fourteen, but this certainly wasn't my first full grown hangover. In the middle of the droning sermon, I'd rested my head on my hands, elbows on my knees. Our pastor's nasal voice lulled me from the pulpit into that state somewhere between sleep and wakefulness. I'd rested my eyes for only a moment. Bang! Searing pain exploded through my forehead, and my heart rate immediately shot through the roof as I awakened in full fight or flight mode. I thought I had been clubbed, but as I looked up, everyone—including my parents, the pastor, and the entire congregation—stared at me. I'd fallen asleep, my elbows had slipped from my knees, and my head had crashed into the wooden pew in front of me. I hated being forced to go to church.

"I clearly should have gone more," I concluded.

He smiled a sort of weary understanding grin and confided, "I'm not really sure that's how it works."

When I said nothing, he said, "I sense a little anger there. Angry at church or angry at God?"

"Both."

Pastor Wray let that marinate. He was patient. He seemed to understand. After that day, he visited each Wednesday. I allowed him in to see Joan when he asked, but mostly he visited with me. Maybe he sensed my desperation. Whatever the reason, his friendship touched me at a time when I felt even more isolated and marginalized than Joan. We sat and talked for hours about many things, but mostly just about life. He was the first pastor I had ever known who celebrated his weaknesses—a far cry from the pastors of my youth who wore their perfectly righteous façade like a shield. I knew better. I knew some of their dirty little secrets, some of which would have gotten them kicked out of our little conservative church. They were no better than me—maybe worse, in my view, because of their hypocrisy. I at least was upfront about my sinning. Pastor Wray was honest about his past and present, too—the first person to help me understand the debt I wrote about in my piece on surrender did not have to be repaid. God wasn't keeping a tally. The first to introduce the idea that maybe God wanted me broken, nothing left to rely on but Him. He was the first person to let me know that Joan's illness and Alex's tenuous condition were not because of me.

17

Home

A month after Joan's diagnosis, with an odd sense of déjà vu, we arrived back at our front doorstep. Her induction round of chemotherapy had come to an end. Her body had responded as it was supposed to, her bone marrow and her immune system had become a barren wasteland, a place where we hoped they would begin again with growing healthy cells, not the malformed cancerous ones that had taken over her system. Joan was weak, though, and had been given a short two weeks to heal and collect herself before another long month of consolidation chemotherapy. Our month away from home had seemed a year. Our ears—which had become accustomed to the constant background noise of monitors, intercoms, and IV pumps—were suddenly left with little to hear. Joan hadn't really even smelled fresh air, free from antibacterial soap and medicine, since she had taken that long, lonely ride in her ambulance. We both longed to at least act as if we were a normal couple again, even if only for two weeks. And Joan didn't waste a second—immediately planning a Thanksgiving gala rivaling a royal court festivity to celebrate her homecoming. Just her thing.

"Don't you think we should just have a low key affair? Maybe just the two of us?" I suggested.

Joan replied, "I was thinking more like Matt and Jodie, Brian and Susan, Todd and Michelle, Randy and Jackie, and your mom and dad, my mom and grandmother."

I was not at all interested in a repeat performance of the lightning fast infection that nearly killed her during her first round of chemo. People meant germs. Germs, with no functioning immune system, meant infection. Infection to Joan likely meant death.

I tried to let her down easy. "No, I'm sorry, Hon, but I can't even consider that."

"I don't see how it could hurt."

"I can think of a million ways it could hurt. Do you remember at all the night in the ICU?"

"Actually, not really. I'll be careful."

She said it in her hurt little girl's voice, and I knew I had pushed too hard. I was walking a tightrope attempting to divine her feelings while still being honest.

I didn't at all enjoy the role of gatekeeper to my wife's company, but I felt forced into it. Joan had never been particularly interested in following directions as they pertained to her prior to her diagnosis. Other people following rules? Yes... but not her. She'd played along while captive in the hospital, but I feared she would slowly relax the regimen meant to keep her well while home and without supervision. On the other hand, it was her life and her illness—who was I to interfere with her wishes in what could be her last days?

A moment later her demeanor changed drastically. "I'm so glad to be home!"

She jumped around like a little kid with her arms in the air.

"I'm glad too, Love. How 'bout we plan Thanksgiving dinner with just my parents and your mom and grandma?"

"Can we make it formal?"

"Yes, we can make it formal."

"Can I decorate?"

"Yes, you can decorate. I'll shop and cook if you'll help me plan the menu."

"Eight courses?"

"Yes, eight courses."

"China?"

"Of course."

"Individual salt shakers?"

"Yes, if you can find them. I can't honestly believe you have miniature salt and pepper shakers for each place setting. Only you..."

She balled up her fists and threw them in the air and again began bouncing around the room saying, "Yay! Yay! Yay! Look at me. I'm Tigger. I'm bouncy-trouncy-flouncy-pouncy-fun-fun-fun-fun-fun. The wonderful thing about Tigger is I'm the only one!"

She was truly "the only one."

The night of the banquet, Joan was in her element, barely able to contain her joy. Shimmering in her royal blue velvet dress, the scar on her neck and above her breast covered, she glided around the table waiting on our guests as if they were her only care in the world. Cheeks flushed with emotion, not the cherry red color that was the telltale sign of infection or fever, but the "I'm alive and happy" color of red, as she directed the ceremonies. I marveled as Joan transcended her illness and forgot for the moment that she even had cancer. We were players in her favorite movie, "Cinderella." With a little bow at each table setting, she served the sparkling apple cider. With each return to the kitchen, a little curtsy and a blown kiss before disappearing. Her eyes sparkled, her teeth shone, her dimples—on glorious display. I imagined her twirling about in my arms as the orchestra played. Waltz upon waltz, we danced. I sensed the party might well be our last together. I wanted the evening to be perfect.

The evening was indeed magical, but soon enough the clock did strike. An Air Force medical evaluation board (MEB) had convened after Joan's diagnosis to determine if she was or ever would be fit for duty again. For some reason, the usually extremely inefficient military complex worked with supernatural efficiency in our case. Within days, Joan was found to be a detriment, and the Air Force moved quickly to discharge her from active duty. A friend who'd been a part of the proceedings called to tell me.

Without preamble, he said, "They're going to board her out."

"Fuck! How in the world did they decide that? Is it final?"

"I thought you'd ask that. Not yet, but you'd better hurry."

While under other circumstances, a discharge would have been Joan's dream, this decision felt catastrophic. I immediately jumped to the conclusion that Joan would be left with little or no medical benefits—that we would be responsible for finding an insurance company willing to accept her and her preexisting cancer and pregnancy with a likely compromised baby and a long-term NICU stay. Impossible.

I scrambled to think of a way to influence the board. My wife had spent the better part of six years repaying her debt to the Air Force for her medical school scholarship. Her tenure had been extremely taxing emotionally, but she'd persisted and finally even become an integral part of the team she had so loathed as a resident. In spite of her neg-ative feelings, she was the first to volunteer to deploy to Afghanistan after the September 11, 2001 catastrophe. She had not gone, though. No one from Travis had. She was the only anesthesiologist to volun-teer around the clock coverage in the hospital while the base was on lockdown, and she continually offered to go above and beyond what most of her peers were willing to do, just because it was the right thing.

My first call was to my old friend, Kathy. She knew about Joan's diagnosis, but she knew nothing about her career predicament.

I started with, "Kath, I have a problem."

Her reply, just as simple, "What is it?"

"They're boarding her out."

"What? No way."

"Way. Are you still in touch with PK?"

PK was our old commander. He was also the retired major gen-eral trauma surgeon that we'd worked with at Wilford Hall through so many long nights on trauma call. He was also the former Air Force Surgeon General.

I didn't have to tell her what to do. She knew how to fix the situ-ation if it was possible.

I also began planning initial contact with the producers of each popular national morning news show. If forced into a corner, I planned to come out with overwhelming force. To tell the sad story of a young Air Force Major, pregnant, and newly diagnosed with leukemia—how she had been among the first to volunteer to deploy to Afghanistan and Iraq, and that after all of her service and with all of her problems, the Air Force was going to deem her unfit for duty and discharge her with nothing—no medical benefits or retirement at all. I believed some major network would surely be interested in a human interest story like ours.

Next, I informed every relevant Air Force administrator that our story would be on the morning news if Joan was, in fact, discharged without medical benefits. I still loved the Air Force, but I now had little time for the mid-level bureaucrats that held our lives in their hands.

After a week of conniving, I got another call from my friend.

"Hey, Buddy, call off the dogs. They reversed their decision. She'll be medically retired. Much better."

"What dogs?" I asked with as much innocence as I could muster.

"What did you do, anyway?"

"Do you really want to know?"

"I'm not sure. Do I?"

"Well, for one thing I called Kath."

"Enough said."

"Yup."

Then he suggested we have a drink to celebrate, but I had a memory of polishing off three bottles of wine by ourselves one night before I was on trauma call the next day. That was not a good memory. Old times were not necessarily good times. I was no longer that guy, and I asked for a rain check.

Our life at home became pleasantly but bizarrely mundane once more following the medical board scare. Joan puttered around the house thoroughly enjoying dusting, rearranging, reading for pleasure, eating the food we prepared together, and spending time in the room that would become our nursery—domestic things that brought her great comfort. We enjoyed visiting with family and a few friends who had come to visit, disregarding my negative feelings about company. We still erred on the side of caution when near strangers and mostly remained at home attempting to heal as quickly as we could—resting both our bodies and minds to prepare for the coming onslaught of another round of poison.

Though we were home for those two weeks, Joan was nonetheless required to begin intrathecal methotrexate treatments—chemotherapy placed directly into her spinal canal—to prevent cancer cells from invading her spinal cord and brain. She was able to receive these treatments at David Grant, which was only a mile from our home, instead of UC Davis which was forty-five miles away in Sacramento. Carolyn, Joan's cancer specialist and friend who'd been waiting for me that first night of our cancer journey, quickly became a large part of our lives during this round, providing reams of information about leukemia and specific treatments. She was also responsible for a gift I can never repay; she allowed me to administer Joan's methotrexate.

Intrathecal methotrexate must be administered through a large needle inserted directly into the spinal canal. Hematologists aren't—by any stretch of the imagination—experts at accessing a patient's cerebral spinal fluid with a spinal needle. To overcome their lack of finesse, they often opt for brute force and use larger, more rigid needles which, in turn, cause more damage to the tissues they travel through. The procedure itself can be fraught with side effects from even the best technical provider. Carolyn recognized that I, who had performed literally thousands of spinal punctures by then, would be willing and able to administer Joan's chemotherapy with much less chance of the extremely painful post-dural puncture headaches that often occur with less refined methods. More importantly, she recognized the gesture might allow me to feel like an integral part of Joan's treatment. I quickly agreed. She was right.

Grateful but terrified, my hands shook as I stood over Joan's naked back. Her skin was an orange-ish brown color from the betadine I had just painted liberally over the area covering the lumbar vertebrae that were threatening to break through her friable skin. She had lost so much weight during her first round. I hadn't really noticed until I saw her frighteningly frail body hunched over the treatment table. Her face had conversely gained fullness while on a regimen that included steroids. Her frailness was usually disguised by her clothing and fuller face. With only a flimsy hospital gown, open in back, her iliac crests were visible, too, even with her pregnant belly which should have been much bigger than it was. My fingers tremored slightly as I drew into my syringe the local anesthetic that would numb her skin and tissues through which I would insert the five-inch needle. Caroline hovered over my right shoulder. I couldn't tell if she was just curious, or whether she was as nervous as I felt. A small bead of cold sweat inched ever closer to my beltline in back. I was frightened of causing her harm in some way, but by then, I was an expert in hiding my anxiety. My face was all business.

I remembered the time in Joan's bedroom the night after I had a hernia surgically repaired. That night, when the numbness was wearing off, Joan offered to give me a shot of Toradol that we'd been given as post-op pain medicine. As she lowered the needle toward me, I freaked out. I had never been afraid of needles, especially a very small one like this. But somehow, the thought of Joan jabbing a sharp metal object into the muscle on the lateral part of my thigh was more than I could take. I wondered if this was at all like that for her. Or was it just part of life? She was so calm. Or was she just like me, placid on the outside, turmoil beneath?

"Here comes the pinch, Hon."
"Okay."

"Here goes."

She sat perfectly still, whereas I had almost jumped off the bed in our previous role reversal.

"You're so much stronger than I am," I said with more emotion than I had intended. Carolyn faded into the background. "You should only feel pressure now."

The words would not have seemed intimate, but our emotion was palpable.

I felt awkward talking an anesthesiologist through a procedure she had performed hundreds of times, but I felt her need to be soothed by my voice, if not my words. I was soothed, too. The words were part of my procedure. I said them without thinking—as I had thousands of times before. I felt the faint pop as my long spinal needle punctured Joan's dura mater—literally "tough mother" in Latin, the last and sturdiest of the seven layers of tissue before her spinal canal. I was fully immersed in the procedure now—something I could do without even thinking, yet I remained cognizant that my patient was also the woman I loved.

"I'm in, Hon."

"I could feel the pop. It was kind of creepy."

"Sorry. Are you okay?"

"Yes, thank you."

Drip... drip... drip...

Her cerebral spinal fluid slowly filled the small vials. The clear fluid was required to drip passively. I wasn't able to aspirate it. I wasn't sure why, but I assumed negative pressure could somehow denature the cells.

Drip... drip... drip...

My mind floated passively as I waited for the vials to fill. The drips reminded me somewhat of an hourglass. The catch phrase from *The Days of Our Lives,* which I'd watched while skipping my college classes, seemed fitting. "So are the days of our lives…" I wondered if those drips truly were as the days of our lives. How many drips remained? How many grains of sand?

18

AMA
(Against Medical Advice)

Along with Joan's methotrexate treatments, during the last week of November, we were required to stop by the obstetrics ward at David Grant for non-stress tests (NST) to monitor Alex's well-being in utero. While each visit felt like somewhat of an interruption in our convalescence, we did at least enjoy listening to and watching Alex's tiny heart thump along. At David Grant, we had the advantage of being acquainted with the staff, which meant skipping most of the red tape and being seen quickly. On the down side, David Grant was by now staffed with only one perinatologist. The big boys in the government Base Realignment and Closure Committee were trying to shut down their Neonatal Intensive Care Unit (NICU) because it was very lightly used in contrast to the immense amount of money required to keep it open. Dr. B., the only perinatologist and head of the NICU, was attempting to prove David Grant's two-bed unit could still compete with the twenty-bed NICU at UC Davis and several others in the San Francisco area. He was literally fighting for his job. Neither Joan nor I liked him on initial evaluation, which was curious. We both liked and got along with most people we met. Dr. B. was young, just out of his post residency fellowship. He maintained a relatively good reputation throughout our medical community and was clearly liked and respected by his residents. Knowing this gave us pause. We were both uncomfortable being in his care. Nothing obvious, just a gestalt. He was a small man; average height, slightly built with the pasty white skin of one who rarely saw the sun. I'm sure he came by his lack of color as a byproduct of the years of school and training he had just completed, but his wan complexion and bookish appearance made him seem untrustworthy to me. Despite my feelings, we were faced with little choice.

One morning, we sat in the triage area—an open bay with several beds, with only curtains for privacy. The bay was empty except for us, so we spread out a bit and kept the curtains open. Joan's nurse quickly and efficiently attached monitor belts around Joan's midsection. They were wide and white with small pink stripes. I wondered if they used blue ones for boy babies. She placed the light blue transducers under the belt and poked the small nipple through a pre-made hole to keep it in place. As she applied the gel to transmit the sound of Alex's heart rate, Joan gave a little grimace because of the cold. Her eyes were exquisitely expressive. Each little crinkle at the outer corner could mean anything from joy to sheer terror. We immediately heard the comforting sound of Alex's grape-sized heart beating away and saw its gentle, wavy, hill-like tracing on the graph paper that was running through the machine and spilling onto the floor.

Most of Joan's NSTs were about an hour long, but this particular one stretched longer. We both noticed and commented to one another. Joan shrugged her shoulders in what was meant to be a carefree gesture, but didn't quite convey her meaning. We had been watching Alex's fetal heart rate tracing for the entire time we had been there. There was really nothing else to do. The triage area had no televisions, and Joan and I had, for the moment, exhausted our interest in conversation. Besides, hearing Alex's heart beat had become fascinating to us. Alex had always been real to Joan, but had only recently become that way for me.

Just then, Dr. B. walked purposefully into our little spot in triage.

"Your baby is having some concerning variables. I'm not going to admit you yet, but I want you to go home and stay on bed rest. Do a kick count every hour."

I could see Joan's look of concentration quickly changing to one of confusion and fear. "Every hour? What happens if one comes out low?"

"Get here as fast as you can."

That seemed stupid. I wondered why he didn't just admit her if he was so worried.

Despite my questions, we left quickly.

"What if she's just sleeping in there?" Joan asked later. We were lying in bed, Joan on her side. Both of us with one hand on her belly hoping Alex would keep kicking. Joan was chewing on her lower lip. I imagined I could feel both of their hearts beating through her belly. Quick and thready for Alex, quicker than normal, but stronger for Joan.

"I don't know, Hon. I wish he had just kept you there."

"What if we fall asleep and miss something?"

"I'll make some coffee for me. You sleep. I'll keep my hand on your belly."

We'd already packed our overnight bags.

Joan dozed fitfully. I was too hopped up to sleep, so I lay beside her, my hand on her protuberant belly, counting Alex's kicks. Wondering how long this would last.

Haggard and drawn after our night, we arrived at the hospital the next morning as instructed. Joan was between twenty-nine and thirty weeks gestation by then. On arrival, she was again attached to a fetal monitor. We studied the screen intently for any specific decelerations that signaled Alex was in jeopardy. Her heart rate tracing soon began to show subtle irregularities, but neither the nurses, nor Joan, nor I became terribly concerned.

Our nurse that day was an older African-American civilian with the air of a doting, Southern mother. We adored her. She sat with us for most of the morning and chatted. She called Joan "honey." Many of the nurses were slightly on edge caring for a well-known physician, and they subsequently came off as a bit awkward. Our nurse that day didn't show even a bit of recognition that Joan was an anesthesiologist. "Just Joan" liked it that way. She felt more comfortable being anonymous.

"Honey, Alex is looking wonderful today!"

"Oh, good," Joan said in her warmest, most positive voice.

Mid-morning, Dr. B. rushed in.

"They're setting up the OR. We're going to do a c-section."

We both said, "What?" at the same time.

"Have you been looking at the monitor?" Dr. B. asked when we challenged him.

I didn't know how far to push it. He was the specialist; I was merely an anesthesia provider who had enough knowledge and training to be dangerous. So was Joan. I was way out of my league and I knew it, but Alex's and Joan's lives hung in the balance. We were caught in a place where both answers could just as easily be right or wrong. Alex was still a very early preemie. Being born might just be the worst thing for her. Then again, Joan's uterus was becoming hostile. We couldn't deny that fact. Neither of us had seen anything to warn us that Alex was in imminent danger, but we had not studied high risk obstetrics for years.

Joan rescued me in the firmest, most matter of fact voice I had heard from her mouth since she refused sedation for her first bone marrow biopsy. "I'm not having a c-section."

"What?" Dr. B. asked, venom in his voice.

Joan calmly said, "If you force the issue, we're leaving."

"And you received your high risk training where?"

"Goodbye, Dr. B."

"You could be killing your child."

She said nothing more, and I was struck speechless, but his horrifying statement sealed the deal for me. All I could think was, "He's an asshole. Why should I put the life of my wife and child in his hands?" I came a hair's breadth from punching him in the face, my anger had flared so quickly. In the end, though, all I did was look blankly back and forth between him and Joan.

Joan's nurse scurried in. She must have been listening on the intercom or out of sight behind the door with the speed at which she appeared. "You're gonna be okay, Honey. So's Alex."

We walked out quickly as we talked. Joan was still an active duty airman and was bound to follow lawful orders. By disregarding Dr. B.'s advice and leaving without his consent or order, we risked being held financially responsible or even being thrown in jail—not to mention the fact that we were only guessing Alex was not in as much danger as Dr. B. let on.

I was shocked by Joan's quick and passionate declaration. Although I was well aware she could be stubborn, I never would have imagined her making a decision against a specialist in the field of high risk obstetrics about the child growing inside of her. I agreed with her, but I was momentarily confused by her verve.

"We need to hurry. I can't feel Alex kick."

I snatched a peek over my shoulder. We were both set on our path by that time, and right or wrong, we would never have turned back. Dr. B. was writing a scathing AMA (leaving against medical advice) note in Joan's chart.

"Are they chasing us?"

"Not yet."

19

Personal Savior

Four weeks later, we watched Joan's regular contractions roll placidly by on the screen. Following our escape from Dr. B., we had driven directly to U.C. Davis where we'd remained ever since, waiting for this very day. While Joan's civilian perinatologist had kindly hemmed and hawed to avoid throwing her military colleague under the bus, she had seen nothing concerning on her initial examination of Joan and Alex, nor in the month since. Joan was being induced for labor this day because Alex had reached the magical number of thirty-four weeks gestation. She was finally considered mature enough to take the chance that being born and living outside Joan's uterus was better for her than remaining inside. Joan was already scheduled for another round of chemotherapy in which her blood counts would again plummet, and childbirth would become much more dangerous, especially in an emergency. This was the compromise we had all made. This was to be Alex's birthday, and Joan had already been contracting and in labor for six hours. An induction at just thirty-four weeks gestation—with her body not quite ready for labor—was a Hail Mary, but with each pleasant little bump on the monitor, our hopes for a vaginal birth became more real.

I wasn't watching the monitor at the exact moment I sensed a change, but I knew immediately. Joan sensed it, too. Her eyes quickly found the all-seeing screen, and just as quickly, they found me. She briefly shed the mask she had acquired during her first round of chemotherapy, and her eyes, wide open, pupils dilated, began to glisten, tears highlighted by the bright hospital bulbs.

We had no time to debate.

A nurse grabbed the head of the bed and ripped its power cord from the wall. A second nurse grasped the foot. Someone threw me a pair of green scrubs and barked, "Put 'em on."

I tore my clothes off, donned my scrubs, and sprinted to catch up, hat and mask in hand. As I drew even with the bed, I desperately grasped Joan's hand.

We crashed through the OR doors, and the nurses literally lifted Joan by the sheets beneath her and threw her onto the operating table. The anesthesiologist, someone I had met briefly as he inserted Joan's epidural, was already at the head of the OR bed to dose her with the medicine that would make her numb from the chest down. I knew exactly how long that anesthetic took to be effective. So did Joan, and she was paralyzed with fear. We both realized the surgeon likely wouldn't wait the five minutes for his medicine to work.

Lawrence Kingery, the stooped old man who lived across the

street from me, was sitting on his chair as I knelt in front of him behind the baptistery of my home church the same night I had felt the Holy Spirit guide me to the front. "Do you, Darrin, accept Jesus Christ as your personal Savior?"

"I do."

"Then pray. Ask Him to come into your heart."

"What do I say?"

"Whatever is on your heart."

He was the first to urge me to leave the rote prayers of my childhood behind and enter into a conversation with God, the first to show me I could feel as if God was a friend and comforter, the first to give me hope that I would someday attain what I had been taught was a mature relationship with Him in which I was able to share my entire life—foibles and all—with no risk of judgement.

Since that day, I had fallen back on the memorized prayers I had been taught to bless our food and protect our sleep, if I prayed at all. I still did not feel comfortable talking to a God I never saw and had rarely felt, but in my fear I prayed. "Dear Lord, please don't let her feel it. Don't let her scream. Let Alex live! Let them both live!"

The scrub tech splashed orange/brown tinted iodine solution on Joan's belly as a disinfectant, a nurse plastered the blue surgical drape over her, and the anesthesiologist clipped it to the two IV poles straddling the bed. He grasped a clear vial of medicine with a yellow top from his tray of anesthesia drugs. The vial contained ketamine. He was as aware as I that the medicine in the epidural wouldn't have time to elicit the desired numbing effect, and he hedged his bets by administering the powerful hypnotic anesthetic drug related to PCP—something I would also have done. He peered over his glasses and showed me the syringe, clearly inquiring if I agreed with his decision to administer a dose of the drug that would undoubtedly send Joan into a bizarre dream world and induce amnesia. She wouldn't remember Alex's birth. I nodded. He pushed the plunger of the syringe to the bottom.

Before I was even able to turn toward the surgeon, I heard her say, "Tell me if you feel anything sharp." I knew the scalpel was on a downward arc toward Joan's abdomen. She was already in an anesthetic induced haze and likely wouldn't feel the bite of the knife, but if I was wrong and she did, she thankfully wouldn't remember. Nevertheless, cold perspiration rolled slowly down my back, and I braced for Joan's scream as the surgeon rushed to extricate our baby. Thankfully, the cry I heard wasn't Joan's. Within a minute, I saw the surgeon's hands probe deep into Joan's abdomen as the scrub tech pushed with the weight of her entire body on Joan's chest. The moment we had waited anxiously for had finally arrived.

A wrinkled, frail creature was pulled from Joan's abdomen, and the surgeon held her aloft. The scrub tech clamped and cut her umbilical cord, a fine spray of blood escaping. Mercifully, her eardrum-splitting screech came. Then the creature extended both arms and legs, and I felt overwhelming relief, a depth of feeling previously unknown to me.

My beautiful wife lay in a semi-comatose state below me—her appearance wan, perspiration clinging to her brow and upper lip, head rocking rhythmically side to side, eyes moving back and forth above the green oxygen mask in a classic Ketamine gaze. Her lips moved, but she made no sound, save an occasional sigh. I scanned the monitors above her to assure myself she was in no danger, kissed her brow, and then walked to the incubator to see the miraculous creature we had named Alexandra.

The nurses swaddled her in a warm blanket to present her to

Joan, though Joan was completely unaware. They then packaged Alex in a mobile incubator for the short ride to the NICU, keeping a running dialogue with me concerning their actions and what they expected from her. They were hopeful, but matter of fact. Alex appeared to be doing quite well, but she was tiny, just 3.1 pounds.

On arrival in the NICU, the nurses immediately guided me to a rocking chair, and I was completely overcome. For a moment, without Joan present, and while the nurses attended to Alex, I was no longer required to be the strong one. Alone in a room full of people busily caring for the miracle who was part me, part Joan, the raw feelings I had pent up for so long broke loose, and my tears surged.

Only after the storm subsided was I able to sit with my child in my arms.

Alex was so tiny, not really much larger than one of my hands. Could this fragile being with transparent skin cope with the world into which she had been born? She was fully awake, searching and absorbing her surroundings, with her eerily familiar brown eyes wide. An overwhelming wave of protectiveness and responsibility crashed through me.

I suddenly knew why I'd been born—why I'd been put in this place—why I'd been chosen to love Joan and by proxy, Alex. And just maybe I glimpsed how God loved me. I gave my heart away that day. Fully.

20

Rituals

And as easily as that, our lives became routine yet again. Joan spent a week in the hospital healing from her surgical wounds and visiting Alex, getting used to being a mother, reveling in her role. In the NICU, I watched quietly each day as my bald, yellow-skinned, battle-scarred wife clutched our baby to her chest. Joan's cancer vanished. Pain and fear were immediately wiped away the instant they touched. Both ceased being separate entities. Joan fulfilled her ultimate destiny, and I knew that if she were to perish the very next day, those moments in the NICU would have made Joan's life and our relationship worth the pain.

Joan was sent home for a brief respite prior to her final round of inpatient chemotherapy. Although we were happy to return home, we didn't relish the forty-five mile commute each day to visit Alex while she remained in the NICU.

As the New Year approached, we browbeat the NICU doctors into allowing us to take Alex home, too. She was still technically below the body weight required for discharge, but we took her with a feeding tube that would remain in place until she was strong enough to suck on her own. We were both capable and willing to feed her in the relative comfort and safety of our own home. We also believed our lives would be much easier for Joan without the requisite drive to and from U.C. Davis. I had been inserting and using feeding tubes for years as a nurse and as an anesthetist. Joan also possessed some experience and absolutely no fear concerning the feeding procedure.

Alex returned home with us on New Year's Eve, 2003. She was so small, we were forced to wedge her between rolled towels in her car seat. Joan sat beside her while I drove white-knuckled the entire way home. Alex still weighed only 3.5 pounds.

As soon as we got home, Joan said, "I'm going to breast feed," one of her statements that left no room for compromise.

We had discussed the pros and cons ad nauseum and finally decided against it, even though Joan had very much desired to, because of the dangers of her chemotherapy entering her breast milk and being passed on to Alex—not to mention the danger of mastitis when she was forced to cease milk production.

She continued, "I changed my mind."

My terse reply was a question. "Didn't doctor G. and doctor V. say no?"

"They didn't give a firm 'no.' I took it as more of a suggestion."

She hadn't received chemotherapy for several weeks, and after studying the metabolism of each drug, she'd deduced that little of the poison would still be circulating throughout her system. She had also discussed the merits of nursing with her heme/onc and obstetrical team. Both were against her plan, but they were not without compassion. She was right. They hadn't given a firm "no," realizing Joan might feel the need to bond with Alex in that way and realizing the act itself was probably not dangerous for either of them.

Joan quickly became obsessed. As obsessed as she had been when trying to conceive. Though she knew Alex still wasn't strong enough to obtain adequate milk to sustain her, she said, "I can't even describe what it feels like to have her snuggle next to me and nurse."

No matter how negative I felt about this, I couldn't help but look on.

Joan curled up with her knees together and to her side on our ratty corduroy couch, light green and white stripped pajama bottoms comfortably wrinkled and worn soft by constant wear. She carefully unbuttoned her matching top, slowly and tenderly, as if the act of unbuttoning her buttons themselves set in motion a ritual that brought her ever deeper into a trance into which I couldn't enter. Eventually, she would peer up expectantly at me and raise her arms to receive Alex. Then she slowly lowered her and held Alex's face gently, but firmly, to her nipple as she cupped her own breast and squeezed slightly to give Alex a smaller profile to attach to.

Though I was mesmerized by the tenderness of this ritual, I couldn't help but be frightened. When I asked, "When are you going to stop?" Joan said, "I don't know. I don't ever want to stop." Her voice was husky and filled with emotion. How could Joan be so sure about the remnants of her chemo? What would happen when she could no longer continue after the commencement of her next round?

Somehow she would have to stop her milk from coming in. A bout of mastitis could kill her.

Though I could never stand up to her tears, in my head, I held a running dialogue...

"God, they're beautiful together."

"But she's going to have to stop soon."

"What about the chemo?"

"What if she gets mastitis?"

"How can you keep her from having this one thing she's dreamed about since she was a kid?"

"She's going to die and leave me alone."

"How am I going to take care of Alex by myself?"

"She's going to be fine."

"Even if she isn't—you owe her this."

"Why do I owe her?"

"Look at your daughter. Her name is Alex. She's a miracle."

[21]

Dedication

Above and beyond newborn baby care—such as bathing, cuddling, and changing diapers—we were still required to stick to Alex's very specific feeding schedule. When Joan wasn't breast feeding, she pumped and saved what little milk she produced. We also stored breast milk from a friend who had just weaned her twins. Along with Alex's hourly feedings, Joan attempted to nurse, and we continued to feed her supplemental milk from a "preemie" bottle to train her. While I imagine caring for a full-term infant is a difficult enough job, Alex's feeding regimen was downright grueling. Each hour we—and to an escalating extent, I—thawed and warmed breast milk to room temperature or slightly above. We then poured a pre-measured amount into a syringe, which we then attached to her feeding tube, trickling the milk into her intestines by gravity—

not forced, due to Alex's still fragile digestive system. Preparation required ten minutes and her feeding an average of twenty minutes.

This process was required each and every hour. During the day, Joan helped as much as her waning energy allowed, but she was not sleeping well, and the lingering wear and tear of her chemo coupled with both major abdominal surgery and the energy drain of breast feeding had stressed her body's healing mechanisms to their breaking point. Each night, I took over entirely.

Alex was fussy and colicky between her feedings. She was also difficult to lull to sleep, so I eventually began putting her on my chest as I lay on the couch. She seemed to enjoy the whoosh whoosh of my heart, and I imagined she was soothed by the sound. I already felt the lack of human touch, but hadn't recognized it as such. Having Alex snuggled tightly to my chest, hearing her breathe, and smelling her scent soothed me also, in a way I had not expected or experienced. I imagined our time together was a small glimpse, however incomplete, into how Joan must have felt as she nursed.

During our respite at home, Pastor Wray suggested a dedication for Alex in the church. Joan and I both felt a need to raise our daughter in a Christian home—me mostly from a sense of duty instilled by my upbringing, and Joan because she desired Alex find the same type of relationship with God that she had come to enjoy.

I remembered the first time we attended a Seventh Day Adventist church after we had moved to California and before we found Pastor Wray and his church. I'd been ill with the stomach flu for three days when we strolled through the front doors. We weren't greeted, so we showed ourselves to one of the middle pews on the center aisle. I fought drowsiness the entire service, and if it wasn't for the way in which the "spectacle" was conducted, I would have fallen asleep, with the real danger of smashing my head on the pew in front of me all over again. White robes for the deacons and deaconesses. All gathered in front by the altar. Gleaming silver plates with flat brown wafers piled on top. More trays with tiny glasses of a dark, red liquid. I assumed grape juice. We had decided to attend church on the day of the dreaded communion. It lasted four hours.

The pastor imparted directions. All with a flourish. "Women are in the room to our right. Men in the room to our left. Families in the back."

I looked at Joan. I'd never attended communion in an Adventist church. She had forgotten to warn me about the foot washing that was a part of it. Just as she had forgotten to tell me about the kneeling for prayer back in San Antonio. I could have gotten over the kneeling, especially once my knee had healed, but the act of foot washing seemed to me too intimate when surrounded by people I didn't know. Joan agreed that that particular church wasn't a good fit for us because of the high degree of ceremony, and we moved on to find the Napa church.

At the Napa Seventh Day Adventist Church, things had begun to change for me… albeit slowly. In this church, we witnessed an amazing mix of contemporary and traditional worship music. Traditional hymns vs. guitars and drums. I didn't care what it was. Music was becoming the gateway to my innermost thoughts and emotions… and maybe my gateway to God. I loved the music. All of it. To the point I was even brought to tears by it. The notes and words struck just the right chord to spawn memories of childhood, teenage angst, and adult love. Pastor Marvin's sermons also had the right mix of realism and hope. Though Joan had never uttered a word, she must have feared she wouldn't be by my side in the future, and I knew she craved this reassurance of my commitment to pass on a relationship with God to Alex. I secretly began to study with Pastor Wray, preparing a surprise for Joan.

The day of Alex's dedication was a beautiful mid-winter day in Napa Valley. Skies clear with a few wispy clouds darting about, casting slight shadows across the stained glass windows on the south side of the church. There were many people in attendance, making me uneasy. They all talked at once until the organ music began with a flourish. Then silence. The assistant pastor ran through the church announcements and added a little commentary. "I think about this, about how often I come to church, how we come in here and we aren't very well aware of what's going on with the people sitting less than ten feet away from us—the pain and joys and sorrows. These people are family. We are a family."

He was referring to us, but also probably to the global church.

I wondered. "Are we a family? I know these people have been praying for me. I feel grateful, but no familial bond. Is this church a family? Will they ever feel like family? I know we are supposed to be. Why don't I feel it? Are Christians family? They certainly don't always act like it. The global church? Religion?"

The service went on. It was Pastor Wray's turn. He nodded to the AV guy in the balcony at the back of the sanctuary. A close-up picture Joan had taken of Alex's tiny little hand in relief as it curled around her own finger appeared on the large screen at the front.

"We have always loved baby dedications in this church, and have waited for this one for a very long time."

I was ready to bolt when he motioned for us to walk up the aisle. I carried Alex, swaddled all in white, including a bonnet. I held her fiercely, not quite consciously protecting her from those many people, all of the danger, all of the angst I had dragged along from my childhood church. I thought wryly, "Waited for a very long time? She's less than three months old." Three months was a blip on the radar in our lives. Then I understood—it was also a lifetime.

"This is such an exciting baby dedication because we've been praying for this baby, this Mommy… and, uh, we've been praying for you, too, Darrin."

I smiled. He had taken some of the pressure off with his irreverent humor.

Joan walked beside me clad in her bright red flapper style hat, head slightly bowed, lips pursed, eyes lowered. She was emotional and somber. Her flowing red dress—which she had painstakingly picked out of a catalog to match her hat—swished as it brushed against my leg. She leaned closer into me as we neared the front.

"Let me see this little creature. Has she reached the six-pound mark yet?"

"Six pounds, twelve ounces." Joan answered immediately—proud of the care we had provided Alex. Even prouder of Alex for gaining weight.

He went on to explain our circumstances to the congregation and kept referring to Alex as "the baby." I found myself screaming inside my mind, "Her name is Alex!"

He pointed to the screen where the picture of Joan's hand with Alex's was displayed.

"To me, that means so much. This morning, we are praising God for a happy, healthy baby here who has doubled her birth weight."

He gestured to the crowd.

"Can we respond to that?" We heard, "Amen!" from every corner of the church. "And just as importantly, a Mom who is doing well in the midst of her third round of chemotherapy."

"We're here today to dedicate this baby to Christ. We're here today to dedicate these parents to raising this beautiful and precious baby—Alexandra Nicole."

He finally called her by name.

"That picture says it all, that baby, so helpless, so out of control, is reaching out and clutching her momma. So, too, do we as a family need to reach out and put ourselves in God's hands. Today we are going to dedicate her."

He looked at me.

"Do you think she'll let me hold her?"

I was reticent to give her up, even to Joan. Our bond had become so strong through the countless hours and dark nights of feeding and cuddling.

But I placed Alex in his outstretched arms.

He prayed the prayer of dedication.

"Today the Dixon family and we at the Napa Church dedicate ourselves to role modeling this family and this precious gift to the best of our ability and dedicate her to You today. In Jesus' name. Amen."

Pastor Wray handed Alex to Joan and gave me a certificate of dedication. He hugged Joan.

"Joan, there's another part of this dedication today."

A look of surprise crossed her face.

"Darrin wants to make sure that you know this family is always together as one."

Her eyes softened. I was looking directly into them. There was no one else for the moment. Even Alex was forgotten. The tiny, little wrinkles appeared at the corners of her eyes, and she lowered her head. I saw her left cheek glisten and the very edge of her mouth quiver.

"Today, Darrin is joining our church."

While I had been uncomfortable with the people and the pomp and circumstance, while I didn't feel I needed to make this public stand, while my public declaration didn't erase years of guilt and angst perpetrated by the church, Joan's reaction to my surprise made the entire thing worthwhile.

[22]

Consolidation

Joan weaned herself one week prior to her second round of chemotherapy. A few days later, she became shockingly ill—febrile, aching, and haggard.

Emergency rooms are frightening, especially to someone with no functioning immune system.

Fearing the worst, we walked through the double doors and into our own special hell. Every nook and cranny filled with sniveling, coughing pieces of raw flesh. I imagined millions of rogue bacteria poised in the air, hovering like miniature apache gunships waiting to launch their attack. Ushered into a small back treatment room that was rarely used, we huddled face to face, knee to knee. Then she rested her head on my shoulder. I could no longer stroke her hair. It hadn't yet begun to grow back. I touched the back of her neck instead and then lowered my hands to her knees. Her body alternately clenched and relaxed as it shook and sought to release her fever. She groaned involuntarily.

At last, the ER physician entered the room. The requisite blood cultures had been drawn. She was soon diagnosed with mastitis, a bacterial infection of the breast sometimes caused by abrupt cessation of breast feeding. Luckily, it was treatable with antibiotics, and we'd caught it relatively quickly.

Relieved outwardly, I was inwardly seething. Joan had wanted her bonding experience with Alex—I got that as much as any man could—but the consequences of her experience were now ominously building like a summer thunderstorm.

"Is this going to delay your next round?" I asked.

She tearfully replied, "I don't know, Honey. I'm sorry…"

And immediately, my heart softened. Her childlike voice in moments of sadness and fear had that affect me. An apology, too. I wasn't able to remain angry with her, especially not now.

Joan's consolidation round of chemo did begin as scheduled the next week. By now, we were practiced at choosing the necessities to transform Joan's small hospital room into a home away from home. While Joan was isolated and allowed no visitors, I cared for Alex with assistance from some generous family members. My mom and dad, Joan's mom, her brother Todd and sister-in-law Sonja, and Joan's dad arrived with his new wife. All in short succession. With that boon of assistance, I fit in as much work as I could.

Using the skills my mother had taught me and relying some on trial and error, I donned the dual hats of both father and "mother." By providence, I had always been sensitive and perceptive, eager to learn and understand not just males but also females. I'd gravitated toward nursing, not just as a route to becoming an anesthetist, but because caring for people came naturally to me. Having grown up with a strong mother, two sisters, and scads of female cousins, I had been near women my entire life. Diapers were nothing for me, feeding babies easy, and holding them child's play. In short, I was comfortable with activities a typical man who had grown up in a traditional Midwestern family might not have been comfortable with. I was also much too proud to imagine not fulfilling both roles. I wasn't angry because of my dual roles, but I was stubborn. I had been raised to believe I could do anything I desired with a little hard work and persistence. I bought in. Raising a baby was nothing different to me than learning to ride a bike or hit a baseball or learn anesthesia—just something else to perfect. I was good at perfecting things.

My life became ever busier, running an OB anesthesia program, taking care of Alex, taking care of Joan, and attempting to keep our home in respectable order. Our house guests had all come and gone, and I was now left fending mostly for myself except for the occasional weekend visit from Joan's mom while I worked. Working actually became more restful than being at home. At work, I was only responsible for my patients, and loosely at that. While I was performing a procedure, I was 100% responsible, but after that, the nurses took care of most everything else. I was free to chat with the staff, talk on the phone, or even glance at the television—something I hadn't done in months. We didn't even own a TV at home. I wouldn't have had the time to watch, anyway.

The administrators at Sutter Delta had been quite understanding, but I worried that their charity would soon end. My practice couldn't go on indefinitely with me always one foot out the door, waiting for the next emergency to tear me away. I actually felt quite replaceable at that moment—for the first time in my life—which was not a good feeling for me. California was also expensive, and on my tenuous salary, it would be difficult to live and care for Joan and Alex.

Meanwhile, my relationship with God—as personal counselor, healer, and friend—was following the same tortuous course as Joan's illness. Easy to believe that God would cure Joan when she was on an upswing. Easy to believe He was my friend and counselor then. When it got bad, though, I slipped into despair, thinking He didn't care or that I hadn't yet reached the quota of prayers for Him to swing into action. Eventually, toward the middle of her consolidation round, I finally found myself in a quiet moment in the rose garden outside the hospital praying in a quiet whisper: "Dear God, I have been a miserable human being. I wished for my wife's death what seems like eons ago now. Please don't let this be an answer to that stupid selfish prayer! I am guilty of being resentful of my precious daughter, the one I now hold so dear, for 'forcing' her way into our lives. I have been resentful of my beautiful wife for talking me into having a child only to threaten to leave me alone. I have been angry that she puts everyone else's life above her own. I am pissed at you, God, because you allowed this and you have not seen fit to fix it. Please change my heart, oh God. Please cure Joan. I am lost Lord. I need your help."

With my feeble newfound faith, I suddenly found hope.

In my spare moments at home, I researched the best cancer centers in the US. The University of Nebraska Medical Center was listed as one of the thirteen best centers in America—this held significant promise for us. My family lived in Iowa, approximately a three hour drive from Omaha. They would be much more accessible and able to help when needed—a short car ride instead of a flight. Also, Joan had been raised there.

We discussed Omaha while lounging side by side on Joan's little adjustable hospital bed.

"What do you think about Omaha?" I asked.

"I love the idea." Though she said "love," she was far from portraying the spirit of the word.

"I'll bet you'll have tons of friends that want to visit you."

"That will be nice."

Not getting the deeper, more honest feelings I was looking for, I changed tactics. "UNMC is one of the thirteen centers of excellence for cancer care in the country. Offutt Air Force Base is there."

Having an Air Force Base nearby was a very big added bonus. Alex and I could still be seen by the Air Force doctors for free, and though I'd recently battled the system, I'd lived on or near an Air Force Base for the last twelve years of my life. I still gained comfort from having something as regimented and familiar nearby.

Increasingly optimistic, I began searching for a job in Omaha. I found out about a newly developed group of ex-military anesthesia providers—one of whom had been my friend in anesthesia school nine years prior. In fact, she and I had graduated number one and number two in our class. The job was to provide anesthesia for a new orthopedic surgery center—one of my favorite types of anesthesia. A day after talking to Lynn, I got a call which I felt certain was a gift from God.

"Hi Darrin, I'm John, one of the anesthesiologists at the Nebraska Orthopedic Hospital. I hear you might be interested in a job. I already know the basics about you. I just want you to know I've already talked to the other CRNAs and my partners. We'd all like you to join us and want you to know that you can have as much time as you need to be with your wife and daughter in the beginning. We won't even be operating for quite a while, just spending most of our time setting things up. You'll be on salary, so you'll get paid, even if you aren't there much at first."

I told Joan the news. "I got a job."

"Hallelujah. I was worried. Not," she said with her mischievous face.

"Yeah, I can see that."

Our house had been too expensive, and now I was anxious about selling it under less than ideal conditions, but after one very long week, we got an offer. I felt no joy, just one more item crossed off my list. I was still stuck enduring the harsh, mind numbing reality of caring for Joan as she underwent her third round of chemo, struggling to care for Alex, and finding some small level of bonding with her that could transcend the everyday chores we'd become partners in.

Even as I crossed things off my list, I still didn't think I could do it all.

With God or not, I still needed help.

One night before the move, I finally came out with what I'd been thinking, "So what do you think about your mom moving in with us?"

I hadn't been around Sandra that much prior to Joan's illness, and I knew virtually nothing about her. In my experience, contrary to how I had felt when telling her the news of her daughter's diagnosis, Sandra had come to our aid each and every time we called throughout the five months of Joan's battle. But Joan still worried about being in the role of her mother's mother.

"I'm not sure," she said now. "It seems like a set up for a disaster."

"You would know better than I, but what other option do we have?"

"Could your mom come and help?" Joan asked.

My mom was a recently retired nurse of more than thirty years. She was a natural. However, even after we moved to Omaha, she would still have my dad and two sisters with families of their own to help care for. I wasn't willing to ask her to do more than visit when she felt able.

"I don't think she could stand not to help, but I can't ask her to move in with us. Your mom seems like the perfect solution," I said. In the wake of her divorce from Roger, Sandra had moved to California to be near us and her aging mother, Evelyn. She'd landed a job, but it was bottom line data entry that barely paid enough to cover her rent in Northern California. "She doesn't really have a job that she can't leave. I think if we allowed her to live with us rent free and bought her groceries in exchange for helping take care of you and Alex, she would be ahead of where she is now."

Joan was still quite pessimistic.

Hopeful, I coerced her. The sun shined slightly brighter in Joan's dreary room, and our surroundings subsequently became more colorful. Even Joan seemed to sense my hope and brightened. I read my Bible. I communicated more freely with our friends. I finally felt a burgeoning optimism that Joan, such an obviously good person, could be cured. Why would God choose to allow someone so kind and selfless to perish?

Welcome Party

In a matter of weeks, after Joan's chemo concluded, I quit a job I loved, packed up our house, broke Sandra's lease, moved two households with three adults, one premature infant, one giant schnauzer, two cars, and more stuff than I ever imagined possible across the country, moved into a temporary apartment, planned to buy a new house, started a new job, and prepared Joan for a lifesaving/life threatening stem cell transplant. Oh yeah, I parented Alex, too.

My ever-helpful extended family descended upon Omaha like a bunch of carpenter ants during the Easter holiday to help move our more essential things into our apartment. We moved everything in a day. In addition to my mom and dad, I'm not sure how many of my uncles, aunts, cousins, and sisters came, but we would have been in deep trouble without them. Family had been one of the primary reasons we moved back to the Midwest, and they had already earned our heartfelt gratitude.

We were cramped in our new living space—having been unrealistic about living with a small infant who required special care, a sometimes helpless mother-in-law with tons of stuff, our large needy giant schnauzer who had been living with Sandra since Joan was diagnosed, an immunocompromised cancer patient, a regular guest appearance by my mom, and my attempts to orchestrate the entire business inside 600 square feet. Yet, as difficult as the move was and as cramped as we felt, we were glad to be moving on and soon found a reasonable routine.

My job hadn't yet begun, but I oriented while Joan was shown around the University of Nebraska Medical Center. I became acquainted with colleagues at my new workplace and Joan with her new care staff. She especially connected with her coordinator, Katy, but they were all great—all very matter-of-fact about the difficult job they performed. Their straightforward demeanor inspired a high level of confidence in Joan.

On the home front, we experienced a second honeymoon of sorts. From the end of April through the beginning of May, normalcy seemed within our grasp. We took daily strolls in the park across from our little town house, watched movies in an actual theater, and spent hours lounging on the shore of a small local lake watching hot air balloons rise into the afternoon sky. We rode bikes, kayaked, and went to our new favorite restaurants—Thai, East Indian, and of course, pizza. Joan loved the pizza from a little chain in Omaha which we ordered to go so we could eat and play games at home on Friday nights. Scrabble was still our game of choice, and each Friday evening, we waged epic battles.

Joan's hair was even growing back, although this time, it was coarse and kinky curly. Our life became normal enough to attend a welcome party at my new boss's house. Joan was more excited than I was. I had become somewhat of a recluse by then and didn't relish large crowds, but Joan used the party as an excuse to shop. She was like a child on Christmas morning as I accompanied her to all of the finer shops in Omaha. I was actually pretty dubious about the caliber of shopping we might find in our new hometown, but she dragged me from cute boutique to cute boutique. Like the sun, she still attracted everyone to her, even conspicuous as a cancer patient with her hair just now beginning to grow. She also sported a rosy glow to her cheeks and her most endearing childlike smile.

"God, I love her...," I thought as I watched her trying on outfits, spending an enormous amount of money on clothes she would likely never wear.

I said it in my head, but she heard me and placed her hand on my cheek, brushing her lips against mine.

"Thank you, my darling. I love you, too."

The night of the party, we pulled up to John's (the chief anesthesiologist's) home and immediately both laughed.

Joan exclaimed, "They're living in our house!"

"I wonder if they know?"

"Do you think he'll be upset?"

John and his wife's house was the exact same floor plan as ours and painted the very same color of dark brown. Clearly the same builder. The only difference—theirs was on a golf course.

"From what I know of John," I said, "he won't mind a bit. I have no idea about his wife."

"Does it seriously have to be the exact same color?"

I was not expecting a lot from this party. The main reason I was there was for Joan. I couldn't deny her the opportunity to get out in a new/old city on a gorgeous night. But I was heartened as soon as I entered their kitchen.

Garlic and butter scent filled the air along with the sweet, slightly sharp smell of good balsamic vinegar. A woman stirred something over the six burner commercial Viking range with a gigantic hood. Red wine stood decanted on the counter. Piles of hors d'oeuvres waited strategically around the room: stuffed mushrooms, canapés, crostini with bruschetta or olive tapenade, and caviar. I spied high end wine on the rack and an intricate Italian espresso machine that was fine enough to elicit my jealousy. Joan was giddy. I was beginning to think, "I may enjoy this party after all."

A long table was set on the grass in the back yard in the deepening twilight. I was reunited with my friend, Lynn, and we got to know the other CRNAs and anesthesiologists. The night was beautiful. Joan and I visited more in that one evening with people other than ourselves than we had in the last six months. Conversations flowed as easily as the wine. Joan politely accepted a glass, but didn't take a sip. She didn't need it, nor did I. We were drunk with happiness. These people were like long lost friends. It was as if we were back in the vaulted basement of the V. Sattui winery in Napa before Joan became ill. Large roughhewn wooden tables spaced around the cavern. Joan in her long silk evening gown and jewels, hair piled in a spiral upon her head. Me in my tuxedo hobnobbing with the president of the California Medical Association and his wife. A formal eight course meal put on by the winery. Joan glowing as she glided around the room visiting with this person and that. The wine, the food, the heady feeling of being slightly intoxicated in the presence of important people.

———

Too soon, the evening came to an end. Darkness had fallen, and our conversation tapered off. We took our leave and slowly navigated our way home, first driving through John's neighborhood, then finally the few blocks more to our identical new house that we still weren't able to move into. We chuckled again as we pulled into the driveway. We didn't yet have the keys, so we sat in our car, basking in the warm comfort of a beautiful evening, wishing things were different, hoping that they eventually would be. Hesitantly, we returned to our everyday lives in our small, crowded apartment.

But as we prepared for bed later that evening, my stoic wife hunched over, clutching her chest. Within minutes, she was grunting and gasping violently for breath.

[24]

Chaos

Just like that, we returned to the hospital, and chaos, and the unknown.

The specialists wasted no time being kind. They poked and prodded and x-rayed and listened for the next several hours until eventually, we were given the news we had feared. Joan's leukemia had come screaming out of remission. The cells in her sternum were replicating and expanding so quickly, Joan felt as if they were about to burst through her chest.

The cancer center kindly allowed Joan and me a double room so I was immediately able to take up residence beside her.

Close to midnight on our first night back in the hospital, I heard rustling in her bed. I was a mere five feet away, senses on high alert, but Joan had pulled back the sheets and struggled to rise before I had a chance to reach out. She was surprisingly quick, even though her equilibrium was off. She managed to force herself drunkenly upright, then fought to stand, relying heavily on her wheeled IV pole. With one step, she lost her balance, reeled to the far side of the room, caromed off the wall like a pinball, and sprawled sideways into the bathroom. I was out of bed, not close enough to stop her, but close enough to witness her fall against the bathroom wall. She struck her head and slumped to the floor. I rushed to her and held her. As I pulled the emergency cord, tears rolled down my cheeks, until finally the nurses arrived.

Joan lost her mental acuity and judgment shockingly quickly, becoming forgetful and seriously confused—especially as darkness fell upon our room each night. I watched powerlessly as the most intelligent and independent person I had ever known became entirely helpless in the blink of an eye. Joan's caretakers had been cautiously optimistic to this point. Coming out of remission had been a significant setback, but an overcomeable one according to them. I don't believe they expected this magnitude of decline. Even they were shocked. I could see the telltale creases of doubt in their eyes and hear it in their increasingly clipped and distant speeches. At the time, I was too shocked to even analyze Joan's chances. I could only sit by in stunned silence.

On the day of Joan's stem cell transplant, I again felt an odd sense of déjà vu. The small fifty-milliliter IV bag on the pole looked tiny, innocuous even.

I was still hoping her transplant would be a miracle, despite evidence to the contrary.

I lay beside her in bed just as I had during her very first dose of chemotherapy so many months ago and even before that, in her dark room while we were still dating. She curled up and faced away. I enveloped her with my much larger body. She was the little spoon, as she referred to the position. I was the big spoon. She felt so frail, so like a small bird.

It was mid-afternoon, and she was as mentally clear as she had been since before her fall, and I held on to our sweet, but indeterminate time together, hoping she wouldn't slip away from me again.

She whispered in her smooth, infinitely kind voice, "Will you marry again?"

"I don't know, Hon. Must we talk about it now?"

"I'm dying. We both know it. You'll find love again, won't you? Please?"

"I can't even imagine my life without you, Joan."

"Promise me you'll marry again. You'll need someone to help you. Alex will need a Mom."

I hesitated for a long while before finally hesitantly replying, "I promise…"

Joan then launched into a description of her friend, Loy—the friend she'd gone to see in Montana, before she'd gotten pregnant, before this nightmare began—as if sowing seeds for my future, not hers, was what mattered.

The stem cells were infused over an hour. Joan and I lay silent for long periods. Her future slowly transfused through a tiny catheter in her arm, mixed with her blood, and flowed through her veins, each beat of her heart circulating someone else's cells throughout her body. Every beat brought her nearer to cure or death, yet she felt nothing. When the IV bag was empty, she slept. I lay awake, calmed by the subtle sound of her breathing—each rise and fall of her chest—but unable to drift off. I could just see the right edge of her serene half-smile as I curled around her from behind.

And I prayed:

"Dear Lord in Heaven, you have the power to cure her. Please don't give us hope just to take it back. Please, please, let her live. Please cure Joan." And then I voiced for the first time what had been bouncing around in my head since Joan's diagnosis. "If you won't see fit to do that, please help me know how to help her die with dignity."

[25]

Train Wreck

Joan and I had discussed both of our wishes regarding life support long before her diagnosis. She believed in being prepared for any circumstance, especially with a baby on the way. She believed that if God wished her to live, He would keep her alive. It was as simple as that for her. I believed in her right to her views, and I agreed with her about not being kept on life support, but for me it turned out not to be that simple.

A week later, Joan awakened from a shallow nap gasping for air. Eyes wide, arms flailing, she lurched forward in bed to grasp every last molecule of oxygen she could bring in. Her color became the mottled greyish color of the dying woman in my dreams. I imagined her team of physicians debating in a huddle at the nurse's station about how to treat her. I knew they were around; I'd just seen them in the hallway making rounds.

I attempted to bring Joan out of her panic.

"Joan, listen to my voice. Slow your breathing down. Look at me. Breathe with me."

Her color was turning from an already sallow yellow color to gray to blue.

"You're going to be okay, Honey. I'm here."

My panic was rising, too, but I fought to keep my emotions under control.

"Nice and easy. In with the good, out with the bad. Slow and regular."

"It's going to get easier. Just a little bit more."

Seven minutes passed. Her condition wasn't getting better, and I could no longer hold my terror in check. I looked frantically around the room for the implements of my trade. Lungs are my specialty. I ventilate and oxygenate patients every day. I am the person to whom people come when a life needs to be saved—the one who can successfully intubate anyone requiring assistance breathing, no matter the cause. In less than fifteen seconds, I would have had Joan asleep, intubated, and placed on a ventilator.

None of my tools were there.

I broke.

Throwing open the door to her room, on my way to the nurse's station to drag one of her doctors back with me, I slammed into one of the residents standing in a teaching circle outside our doorway. I Inserted myself directly into the middle of their little cluster and said, "If you don't sedate and intubate my wife immediately, I will do it myself. With my fucking fingers if I have to."

———

Her symptoms had come on so quickly, I hadn't even had time to debate the ramifications of placing her on life support. I acted out of pure instinct. In our previous discussions, we had imagined the issue to be less messy—something like Joan lying in bed, awake and aware, as her physician asked her tenderly but authoritatively if she wished to go on, if she wished to be placed on life support. This was not tidy. It happened so quickly and violently. It was a fucking train wreck.

I stood alone in the corner of Joan's room—a room filled with doctors and nurses—and felt completely isolated, abandoned even by the God to whom I had just pleaded. There were at least ten people there, but all were too busy attempting to save Joan's life to notice me.

Four letters would have ended her struggle, but I'd caved in the panic of the moment. Within minutes, I awakened to the reality of what I'd done. Joan was lying on her bed on life support against her express wishes. I quietly but firmly asked everyone to leave the room so I could face what had just happened.

As she lay pharmacologically paralyzed, sedated, and artificially ventilated—clinically dead for all intents and purposes—I prayed to God in a totally unguarded way, too exhausted and confused to hold back. "I have nothing left, God. You've taken it all. I tried to help, but clearly I've made a mess of it. I love her, but I can no longer do this. She's yours. Your choice. Life or death."

I desperately wished for God to decide in my stead. I couldn't bear to be the one to kill my wife by uttering the word "stop." But I heard nothing, so I reached out to my only remaining source of comfort.

The time was just after midnight. I stood at Joan's bedside and called my mom.

"Hi, Bud." Her voice trembled.

"It's over, Mom. She will die tonight."

"She's not gone yet?"

"No, but I have to tell them to stop her life support. I have nothing left."

"I'm so sorry, Bud. Maybe there's still a chance?"

"No, there's no chance."

Next, I spoke to Sandra, and with that chore accomplished, I felt more prepared to make the final call—remembering Joan's absolute certainty that God would care for her whether living or dying, in that moment choosing to believe it, too.

As I turned to beckon the care team back into her room to remove her from life support, Joan squeezed my hand. My breath caught in my throat. Her movement impossible. The paralytic administered by the anesthesiologist couldn't have worn off yet. Undoubtedly physically and mentally exhausted—I hadn't slept in my own bed for as long as I could remember, I hadn't slept at all in days—I couldn't have been more emotionally unstable. However, I felt her squeeze my hand, a strong and deliberate squeeze, and I assumed God had just taken control, relieving me from the guilt of having to make the final decision alone and allowing Joan to say goodbye.

"Goodbye, my love," I said. A light kiss for each eye, then her lips, savoring her lingering warmth for the last time.

But within minutes of letting the care team back into the room, within minutes of removing her from life support, Joan's blood pressure began to rise. The doctors and nurses glanced furtively from side to side. Within thirty minutes, Joan stabilized to her pre-crisis blood pressure and was taken to the ICU for monitoring. By morning, she was ready to transfer back to the oncology unit still pharmacologically paralyzed, sedated, and ventilated. But with a heart as strong as if she were a normal healthy thirty-four-year-old. With all my heart, I believed God had finally come through and saved us both from cancer!

Permission

Later that morning, my mom and Sandra brought Alex to the hospital.

Joan was somewhat awake, but only intermittently. She didn't really notice the mothers sitting shell shocked in the corner of the room. She did notice Alex. I was holding her. It had been so long. Her very smell and warmth comforted me, and I sensed that she would be—already was just like—her mother, a sun in the center, drawing people closer.

Joan's eyes softened and sharpened simultaneously, appearing briefly as they once had, but her moment of beauty was cut short as Alex began to scream—obviously afraid of the spectacle that neither looked nor smelled anything like the mother she had known only briefly. Joan immediately withdrew. Her eyes became dull and lifeless.

Her head turned slightly away to the right as she stared uncomprehendingly out the utilitarian hospital window.

Joan was intubated and dialyzed through a venous catheter in her upper right chest for seventy-two hours—too long for the comfort of the people in charge of her care. She was no longer waking up, even intermittently. And I again faced a decision. Joan's doctors were trying to coerce me into allowing them to insert a permanent dialysis catheter and do a tracheostomy. I hesitated. I'd already hedged on any hard line concerning life support. She'd been placed on chemicals to keep her heart working and was intubated and mechanically ventilated. She was also now being fed intravenously. My previous decisions weren't making this one any easier. Should I continue down the life support road? Or should I right my wrong and let her go? My newfound certainty that God was with us vanished just as quickly as my sense of peace had arrived. The only thing I was sure of was the longer this went on, the more difficult the decision to stop would become.

In the absence of an answer from God, crushed that His previous miracle was now proven not to be, I desperately hoped for her to awaken.

One day, a miracle. The next, overwhelming evidence that there was to be no miracle. The rapturous high of knowing God was finally with us and we were with Him… and the soul crushing defeat the next day, believing He had never really been there.

As the sun slowly set behind the parking garage outside Joan's window, she opened her eyes and blinked sleepily.

"Hey, Hon, you've been out for a while. Do you know where you are?" A nursing reflex—assessing her orientation.

She nodded. Her bleary eyes beginning to clear.

"You've had a pretty rough go of it."

Her eyes squinted slightly in what I took as a "You're telling me" smile, even around the plastic breathing tube in her mouth.

I didn't know what she knew or didn't know about her condition at that time, so I hurried to catch her up—not knowing when she would slip again into unconsciousness. My side of the conversation was swift and brutal.

"I don't know what to tell them. The doctors are asking me questions I'm not prepared to answer. I need your help."

She shook her head warily, spurring me on.

"They say it's possible your kidneys will heal. Your heart has already bounced back. Your lungs should come back, but they haven't yet. Not sure why. Your liver is still a problem. They want to try an experimental treatment on you called Defibritide."

Again, a nod. This time slower, more deliberate, sadder. She was fighting to remain in the moment and put order to the immense amount of information I was giving her in such a short time.

"I need to know if you want me to consent to those procedures."

I desperately wanted her to say, "Yes." I wasn't ready to say, "No."

After a moment, she slowly and deliberately nodded yes. She knew what I was really asking—at least that's what I desperately clung to, my ability to read her mind—and the light left her eyes once more. She loved me enough to give permission, or so I chose to believe, making my life easier and hers unbearably longer.

I came up with, practiced, and recited the canned message I prepared for each family member.

"Joan's doctors have asked me to make some decisions concerning her care. You know she took a terrible turn for the worse over a week ago. Her heart failed, then her lungs, then her kidneys, and now her liver. She was placed on a ventilator to assist her breathing, on medications to help her heart pump effectively, and on dialysis to filter her blood because her kidneys are not able to at this time. Joan's doctors feel there is a possibility her lungs will heal if they're allowed to rest. Right now, there is a long tube that goes through her mouth into her trachea. A tracheostomy (small hole in her neck) will dramatically cut down on the length of the tube, allowing her to breathe more easily. It will also allow her mouth to be free of plastic and enable the sores caused by the pressure of the tube to heal. Her doctors also think her kidneys could heal. They were dealt a bad blow by her low blood pressure, but she is young and was healthy before—it's possible they'll restore themselves if rested. The surgeons want to put in a permanent dialysis catheter in her leg. I'm just calling to see if you have any objections."

Their reactions ranged from "Whatever you think is best" to "I'm sorry you have to make that decision." Most of them understood this meant more life support. None had been privy to our previous conversations and decisions concerning life support. None were shocked. No one objected, and even their cursory approval was adequate. I had already made my decision, and it wasn't based on any of their input. I was merely giving them information and allowing them a forum to speak their mind.

Joan's dad, Roger, had once been a medical product representative in Omaha and happened to know one of the "best" ear, nose, and throat surgeons in town. He contacted his buddy surgeon and requested that he examine Joan and perform her tracheostomy. The surgeon agreed.

Witnessing a surgical team prepare Joan for surgery was surreal.

The anesthesia residents arrived en masse to study Joan's chart and examine her. Their exam was cursory as they entered the room and noted Joan's ventilator settings and medications without once laying their eyes on her or touching her. Though I had often performed in the same manner, watching them treat Joan as an object was challenging.

The surgical and anesthesia residents arrived to collect Joan at approximately ten o'clock the morning of surgery. By that time, we'd been waiting for four hours, having been notified the night before that we would be the first case of the morning at seven o'clock with a pickup time of six. I stood in my place at Joan's bedside, holding her hand and doing my best to be unobtrusive. However, obtrusive or not, I was unwilling to let go of her. The anesthesiology resident was too busy disconnecting Joan's various cables and applying her transport monitors to notice me scrutinizing his every move. I scanned the entire team for signs of fatigue, ambivalence, or lack of compassion and sensed all three. I was teetering on the verge of tears and outrage again as the anesthesiology resident connected the small plastic five milliliter syringe—its orange label identified as the same sedative Joan had always refused with her bone marrow aspirations. I was intimately familiar with what was about to happen, and I agonized over my inability to hold to Joan's wishes concerning life support. Her extreme condition made her a terrible risk, and I wasn't at all sure she would live through this procedure.

The junior residents wheeled my wife, one of the best anesthesiologists and clinical instructors I'd ever known, out the door to the hallway, pausing in front of the elevator. While we didn't advertise the fact that we were anesthesia providers, our vocation was well known throughout the hospital, and I guess I was expecting at least an acknowledgement, but the young residents ignored me.

I envisioned the procedure and the operating room. The surgeon would make the initial incision in her graceful neck, rapidly moving through the layers of tissue to find her cricothyroid membrane. Once found, he would look to the anesthesiologist and nod as a sign to slowly withdraw Joan's endotracheal tube in exchange for his shorter tracheostomy tube. If the anesthesiologist withdrew too quickly, Joan's artificial airway would be lost. Her throat could immediately close and make ventilating her very difficult. This surgery was a delicate dance, one I'd attended countless times.

I kissed her softly goodbye. I had no more prayers left. I was less and less sure what role God was playing, if any, in our little drama. I still believed—or rather, more specifically—I still made the choice on that day to believe, despite the mounting evidence in my mind to the contrary.

[27]

The Call

I sat on the floor of her room for what seemed like hours—lonely, cold hours. When Joan finally returned, she looked more like my lovely wife than she had in weeks. Her mouth was tubeless, and I gratefully saw her look of peace as she still slept. The nurses had cleaned her mouth and neck of the old dried blood and iodine, and I recognized for a brief moment a time when she hadn't been ill.

Following Joan's surgery, we waited. Each day began early with the phlebotomists taking their twice daily blood so the results would be done by the time the physicians rounded, then nursing rounds, then the care team with specialists in tow. Later in the morning, physical therapy, sometimes a chaplain, occasionally a short visit from a local friend or one of our mothers. I spent brief respites in the "healing garden," a place where I could get away from the noise and hubbub and rest my ears and mind. In those moments, I missed Alex, but the rest of the time, I couldn't allow even thoughts of her to pass through my mind due to my irrational fear that she too might die or that my steadfast vigil would begin to crumble.

By now, Joan had developed full blown tumor lysis syndrome—as her cancerous cells were killed, they were poisoning her system. Tumor lysis was just one more injury to her already failing system. Small changes in lab numbers meant a good or bad day. Bad days became more frequent than good and enduring the ever increasing intervals between good days was like watching someone drown. Slowly. Agonizingly slowly.

The pulmonary specialists, never willing to give up, still attempted to build Joan's strength. As they slowly weaned her sedation, I noticed subtle signs of change. She wasn't able to move her limbs at all for a significant period of time, but when she finally gained strength and was more able to follow commands, she still couldn't lift her legs more than an inch at the knees. As I diligently assisted Joan with her daily exercises, I became ever more convinced that one side of her body was nearly flaccid while the other was building strength, or at least maintaining. I became convinced she had suffered a stroke. Her care team insisted on additional time for observation. I noticed her pupils were uneven. The team didn't agree.

She started to awaken as her sedation was weaned, and we communicated so effectively, I began to doubt my stroke diagnosis and began to believe she might be making progress.

Assessing Joan's pain was extremely difficult. She'd proven to be much too stubborn to admit she was hurting. The only way I could sense it was by the nearly imperceptible way in which she tensed her eyelids or when her pupils, however uneven, dilated slightly.

I'd gained a significant amount of weight during her hospital stays. I hadn't slept in weeks. Joan's nurses and doctors were dropping comments like, "You should take a break and go home for a while..." I missed Alex like I missed oxygen back in flight school when they purposely made us hypoxic. With her gone, it was like I missed the actual cells that I had donated to her in the beginning. But I couldn't leave Joan for more than a few minutes. I was forced to parcel out my presence, triaging who needed it more. I wondered how long my coworkers would cover for me. Guaranteeing Joan's comfort finally became selfishly about me finding time to rest and regain a little balance. Following a morphine dose, Joan would sleep for a short time which allowed me to walk to the "healing garden" for fresh air without worry. The nurses understood.

One evening, I even arranged for my mom to stay with Joan. My plan was to ensure she was sleeping peacefully before traveling across town to get at least a small dose of Alex's comfort and to sleep in my own bed. I counted on Joan to sleep through the night, but I was unable to shake the feeling that I was walking out on her.

I drove home bathed in the faint orange sodium glow of the freeway, far from fit to drive after having not slept in recent memory. However, I arrived safely and immediately went to Alex's crib to kiss her as she slept. A tiny Joan lying legs and arms akimbo, a blanket haphazardly covering at least part of her body. I picked her up and cradled her in my arms, then was forced to put her back down. My emotions overcame me. I could no longer hold her.

My mattress felt more foreign to me than the hospital cot, but I was so desperate for a decent night's sleep that I just lay there, drifting, locking my feelings for Alex behind a closed door in my brain, enveloped by the warmth and softness of my much higher thread count sheets and fluffy pillow. My reverie didn't last long, however. Within a few minutes of lying down, my cell phone rang. It was as if a remote watcher had been spying on me to see when I finally relaxed, only to use the phone as an electric prod to rouse me out of bed. Joan had uncharacteristically awoken from her sedation and noticed I wasn't with her. Panic ensued, with her frantically pointing to a picture of the two of us on her wall. My mom had no other choice but to call. I had no other choice but to return.

[28]

Goodbye

Joan was definitely not getting better. As her heart, kidneys, and liver continued to fail, the pace of their failure quickened. I had not yet been given any advice from Joan's doctors, yet I could see they were as hopeless as I. They continued to treat her, though, as if she could still pull through. For better or worse, I had inside insight from being in healthcare myself. I knew it was their job to keep treating until there was no hope. I had even seen treatment when there was no hope at all. I had given treatment when there was no hope. I knew they would keep Joan in this state of not quite life and not quite death until I forced them to stop. More than watching for additional signs of Joan's demise, they were waiting for me to break. Waiting for me to say the words. Finally, I called a care team conference and invited both of our immediate families to attend in hopes of getting them to understand Joan's prognosis. I needed the rest of the family to hear what I was sensing from experts. I still needed to hear the words myself. The meeting was held in the conference room on the oncology unit. In attendance were oncologists, PAs, nurses, a liver specialist, pulmonologist, nephrologist, and a cardiologist—all present because I trusted them and knew they would give succinct truthful information about the futility of further treatment.

I systematically asked each specialist if Joan could recover. They all said, "No," but with explanation for the benefit of our family, laying the case for each damning prognosis. My mom winced each time another nail was driven into Joan's coffin, my dad sat stoically, Sonja asked relevant questions, Todd sat with his head bowed, and Sandra stared blankly at something only she could see.

"I'd like you to turn the ventilator off." No one disagreed. Our meeting was adjourned.

I had experienced removal of life support as a nurse. I should have known better than to expect Joan to stop breathing and her heart to cease its rhythmic contractions within moments of unplugging the ventilator. But as she continued to breathe and her heart continued to beat, I hesitated, wondering if there would be yet one more miraculous recovery, one more sporadic intervention from a God I now merely chose to believe in. I knew there was no hope, but still I hoped. Noticing my confusion, one of the nurses reminded me that some patients show signs of progress immediately after discontinuance of life support. The higher doses of morphine they had begun to administer were deepening and slowing Joan's respiratory rate, making it appear she was improving when she wasn't.

She was heavily sedated, suspended—not really alive, but not yet dead, her heart still beating, and her brain stem still sending signals to her lungs to inspire and expire. With each passing moment, I became increasingly impatient—and increasingly guilty for my impatience. My previous wishes for her death now came back to haunt me, and I felt keen remorse. I feared that uttering the final "let her go" or "give her more morphine," would make life after Joan even more difficult.

I sensed the nurses waiting for me to utter some sort of code word that would allow them to actively end Joan's life, but the closest I could come was "Keep her *very* comfortable." And then one day, I spoke with a physician with whom I had become close. She had always been the one able to divine what I was really feeling. Without saying anything different, I believe we chose to end Joan's battle.

Thankfully, she spared me the horror of having to speak the actual words.

That evening, the nurse began administering even higher doses of morphine, but Joan continued to breathe. I wavered, even though I was certain Joan would have come to the same conclusion. I knew she didn't want to "live" this way. I knew the decision would have been easier for her than it was for me, but hope still lingered, just as it had throughout the last nine months.

My favorite nurse came to our room at eleven o'clock PM; we'd been there long enough to call it ours. I was anxious to see her, we had become, if not friends, then something like companions on this journey we had all been on. I wondered how many other patients saw her this way and what toll it took on her. Though she was the charge nurse that night and had many other duties, she'd generously assigned herself to Joan's care. At two o'clock in the morning she entered our room again to sit with me. I was much too keyed up to sleep, sensing this was the night Joan would take her last breath.

"You want to take a walk? I'll sit here with Joan while you go. She's my one and only tonight."

I knew by the look of compassion and sadness in her eyes that she also knew Joan's death was near.

"I really appreciate you looking after her while I'm gone."

"My pleasure, Honey. Is there anything special you'd like me to do while you're walking?"

"Just make her very comfortable."

The same verbal dance, but somehow the words were final that night. I kissed Joan one last time and laid my hand on her chest. I could feel her beating heart, and I soaked in every last bit of warmth and life as I touched her. I walked only as far as the break room. Empty. Hopeless. Forsaken by the great God of miracles.

When I returned home that morning, I found memories of Joan saturating the very fabric of our apartment. She'd died in the presence of our favorite nurse. I'd declined to see her body, preferring to remember the warmth of my last touch over the image and feel of her cold lifeless corpse, but now I found memories of her everywhere. In our simple little bathroom, the few things we'd left behind as we rushed to the hospital that night in May still lay scattered on the counter. I was confronted full force with the simple things she had used every day—a loofah, a pumice stone, and a barely used bar of her favorite soap from which she derived her rich scent. I stood immobile beneath the running water, the first shower I could remember in our little apartment, and hearkened back to our final trip to Maui—how we had showered together. I effortlessly recalled the size, the color of the cold tile, and the fact that it was a walk-in, without doors. There were three shower heads on each of the short sides, and we couldn't resist showering together. I remembered, too, the way she looked every time she stepped out of our shower in California, and how she wrapped her hair in a super absorbent towel, her favorite, aqua green. I even remembered the time I flew from Tampa, Florida, within hours of having major shoulder surgery, to Texas so she could tend to me while my dominant arm was immobile, the way she washed me so tenderly and carefully beneath the soft silky spray of the city in which we'd met. Such a small, utilitarian room, so many memories.

Kindnesses

As Joan and I hadn't found the opportunity to join a church in Omaha, family friends arranged for an Adventist church for her funeral. I wanted to stay true to Joan's wishes. My family wouldn't care about the denomination, but Joan's might. I invited Pastor Wray and his wife from Napa, and they accepted. Their willingness to fly all the way to Omaha on a moment's notice meant more to me than I could express at the time. The Napa church put a collection together to pay their travel expenses.

Facing several hundred people, some of whom I didn't know, in an emotionally charged setting terrified me. I couldn't fathom reminiscing about Joan's life. In fact, I was beginning to feel quite angry—angry at God, the world, Satan, myself, Joan's family, and even Joan herself. Joan had abandoned me, and I found myself wishing I had never met her in that hallway so long ago. I could have been off somewhere with my fellow operators saving someone's life in some exotic part of the world with yet one more unnamed woman to comfort me instead of having to endure the pain of saying goodbye once more to the woman I loved.

I became more anxious as the day of the funeral came closer. Barely able to struggle through the two weeks in between, I might have become hopelessly lost, but for Alex. She literally became the only reason I arose every morning and the sole reason I did not return to my old system of comfort. And the only reason I didn't end my own life. Each morning, I rose to sit with her. Each night, I fed her, played with her, changed her, sat with her, and finally put her to bed. All while Joan's ashes sat in a box on the top corner of my closet—witness to our interactions. The only part about Joan's funeral that I looked forward to was a sense of closure after she was finally laid to rest.

Though I'd never attended this church, the day of the ceremony I found it to be identical to all of the other Adventist churches I had ever entered—strictly utilitarian, a center aisle with angled pews on each side, all leading to a raised platform with a podium in front, a choir loft behind, a baptistery behind that with a large cross, and a piano to the left, an organ to the right. The building itself seemed uninspired, just like the rest of them.

I stood as the dutiful widower in the foyer in a suit I hadn't worn in months, greeting the endless procession of friends and family. Struggling to show some emotion without letting loose the flood, I spotted Joel, Eric, Bob, and Ray, friends from childhood. Unprepared for their presence, I fled to the restroom to compose myself. When I returned: cousins, uncles, aunts, more childhood friends. Joan's group of women friends. Our realtor from California. My cousin,

Kim, who told me tenderly, "If any man can raise a daughter on his own, it's you"—the kindest thing anyone told me during Joan's protracted illness and death. Then the procession of all the military folks so conspicuous with their short hair and ramrod straight carriage. Colonel Kelly, Kathy, Matt, Brian, finally Ken—comrades in arms. Mike was unable to attend. It must have been too painful. The others had come to pay their respects, and all I wanted was to find a quiet corner to sit and hold my baby.

The pastor of the church, who must have felt fairly awkward at having to eulogize someone he'd never met, said a few words of introduction—words I didn't hear. My mind swirled with memories of Joan. Everything blurry. Todd, Joan's brother, played a video montage of her life set to some of the songs she loved. On a screen in front of me was Joan as a child with her miniature schnauzer. She looked so much like Alex. More pictures as she grew into her awkward teenage years, no more ponytails, but now bangs—her eyes so open, authentic, and inviting. My mind wandered, lost in private memories, awash in wistful silence.

Then Pastor Wray walked to the podium.

"Family, friends, and loved ones—we are here to celebrate the life of a beautiful human being."

That was enough for me. I tried my best to keep my shoulders from shaking as sobs wracked me.

Alex, whom I rocked to comfort myself as much as her, began to cry.

Small hands reached from behind and touched me on the shoulder. They beckoned me to hand her back. Helpless, I hesitantly passed my only comfort into my sister Dani's outstretched arms.

[30]

The Waitress

Finnegan's pub was midway between the church and my new house. I entered to the aroma of stale beer, greasy food, and smoke. Nostalgia. I was more comfortable here amongst my fellow miscreants than I'd ever been in any church. The lights were dim and the windows heavily draped, blocking out the evening glow. My company, from several military bases all over the world, sat at a long table in the center. As I approached, each stood and embraced me. They weren't gentle. Too much emotion sparked like electricity through the room. There was no time for gentleness. Several hadn't been acquainted before that day, but they'd all come together without hesitation or thought.

Within seconds, a waitress appeared at my side with a tall, cold beer. She held the frosty mug to my lips as I took my first pull of the sweet nectar. I didn't stop until at least half the mug was gone.

"You're kind of thirsty," she said throatily, teasing.

After she introduced herself I blurted out, "I'm Darrin, and I just buried my wife."

She acted as if my bizarre statement had never been said.

"I'll be over in just a sec with another one for you."

I smiled my best flirtatious smile and immediately felt horrible.

Kathy, queen of bringing up old embarrassing stories, said slyly, "Colonel, remember the night of your party? Darrin asked Joan out for the first time. She said, 'No.'"

Colonel Kelly said, "Joanie really loved that old player piano Beth and I have."

"She loved pianos period," I said. "Did you ever get to hear her play?"

Brian said, "She played in that cozy little bar in Napa. She loved Rachmaninoff."

"Yeah, she loved Rachmaninoff. She had the fingers for him," I said.

I could see her playing at the front of the church. Concentration furrowed on her brow, fingers flying over the keys of the organ. She was playing "The Messiah" for a thousand people. I hadn't known she was a concert pianist when I married her. I should have. Her fingers so sure and nimble, posture so straight and true, her baby grand player piano she insisted have its own room in our house, the way she thrummed her right hand part on my shoulder in a slightly irritating way as we lay in bed talking before sleep, something I already dearly missed.

The bar room became slightly hazy. My head felt off kilter. Not from the alcohol. I'd given up drinking to excess long before in Korea. I'd given up drunkenness easily. When I'd finally committed to Joan, I'd stopped. My commitment not to drink was now magnified tenfold—transferred to Alex. But women were another story. I'd taken my vows seriously, I'd given women up, too, but with Joan gone, wasn't that commitment over?

The waitress came back, sat on my lap, touched my face, and whispered in my ear.

Brian stepped onto a chair, then up to a small four top table, and began undressing to the country music that was playing in the background. I had done my own striptease to "I've Got Friends in Low Places" in a pub somewhere in the vicinity of the Bellagio in Vegas in front of my commander and the entire bar full of patrons one night when we were released from duty at the air show. The night in Vegas was exciting and reckless, this night with Brian, with someone else in the spotlight, felt pathetic, whether because it was not me, or because of the act itself. Matt shook his head. Colonel Kelly left. Colonel Remington drank on obliviously. Kathy let me know that my advances on the waitress were okay.

[31]

Lonely

The next morning, I awoke. Alone in my own bed. But not really alone. The happy babbling and cooing sounds of my reason for living surrounded me, not the boozy, smoky, musky sex smell of a one-night stand. Alex was in her room next to mine. Even through the wall, I was ensnared by her warm voice. For a moment, I imagined waking tangled in a mess of bed sheets and supple female body parts. Just as quickly, those thoughts slipped out of consciousness like a moth—in and out of my peripheral vision—and I was thankful that I had not gone through with it.

I could have stayed in bed, but Alex's happy giggles were irresistible. I went to her room, scooped her into my arms, and carried her to the lime green glide rocker Joan had chosen prior to Alex's birth—which, of course, matched the green in the paint and wallpaper border. We rocked as the sun rose in the east. She fit perfectly—immediately familiar—into my arms. How many nights had we slept on our old ratty couch in California, her tiny body snuggled peacefully to my chest? That day, we sat alone for an hour, and in our closeness, we both began to heal. Through the feel and smell and sound of my child, I began to glimpse God again, through her warmth, and strength, and softness, and unconditional love, and though I couldn't yet forgive Him, I at least no longer rejected Him.

At first, I was anxious about caring for Alex alone, straining against the weight of Joan's ghost peering over my shoulder. I was overly strict, grasping desperately for control, withering under the burden of living up to Joan's ideal. Having missed nearly six months of her life, I hadn't been afforded the luxury of allowing my parenting skills to grow along with Alex. Slowly though, as I became more comfortable and less apt to glance behind for Joan's specter, I did what I knew how to do. I took her for long walks, played in the yard, read to her, and became familiar with the toys she had already accumulated. I began showing telltale signs of parenthood—the familiar rocking motion which never allowed me to stand still again, my one good ear turned toward her distinctive voice, the fear of silence, the relief when I finally put her down to sleep, but the aching longing, knowing I couldn't hold her 'til the next morning. The rest of parenting began to flow naturally, for I was drawn to her, it felt, even more than her mother. She contained the best parts of me. She also contained the best parts, the best memories, and legacy of Joan, and even yet more of herself. Irresistible kinky hair covered her endearingly lopsided head. Her elfin nose and slightly too-large-for-her-head ears. Her mouth, the way the very edges turned up when she was happy and engaged, and turned down when she frowned, so like her mother's, but with her own interpretation. Eyes that squinted in myriad ways, allowing me to read her thoughts just as I had Joan's. I fell deeply in love.

At the same time, my relationship with my mother-in-law became unbearable. We had agreed that she would care for Alex if she awoke in the night during my work week, but I soon found myself awakened while Sandra slept and, with increasing frequency, forced to get Alex out of bed to change her diapers for fear that Sandra wouldn't. Actually getting up and caring for her was not difficult—in fact, I loved it—but I resented that my expectations, our agreements, weren't being met.

I returned each day from work to find dirty dishes and toys lying all over the floor. I was becoming the sole caretaker of my child and my home even with a live-in-nanny / grandmother. Sandra was obviously emotionally bereft. Maybe I should have felt more compassion for her, but at the time, I only felt bitterness, so strong was the drive to get on with my own life.

I had gained over thirty pounds during Joan's pregnancy and illness and now required blood pressure medicine, medicine to sleep, and an antidepressant to relieve at least a part of my suffering. My condition embarrassed and worried me. Alex had already lost one parent, and I felt a rising duty to ensure she didn't lose another. So I began exercising at a local gym. The harder I worked, the stronger, leaner, and calmer I became. Exercise became an acceptable outlet for my raw emotion—suitable for a single father, as opposed to trying to sleep with young waitresses. I loved the feeling of power I gained as I threw weights around, but at home, things were still not improving with Sandra, and I finally felt forced to consider childcare for Alex. A coworker provided a list of nannies in the area, but having someone in the house while Sandra squatted upstairs seemed awkward. I was also worried about the appropriateness of having a live-in female staying with me immediately following Joan's death, as if this mattered more than the appropriateness of attempting to bed a barmaid I met the night I buried my wife. I worried about my ability to keep from seducing a young, naive woman. And what if Alex bonded with her nanny and came to see her as a mother figure, only to have her leave again when she found a better job, or we moved on or, God forbid, I slept with her and we ended things badly? The last thing in the world I wanted was to subject Alex to another loss. Not to mention that finding someone "good enough" for my daughter seemed impossible.

I gave up on the idea of a nanny and, by chance, found a fantastic day care center run by a pediatrician and her husband, an orthopedic surgeon. I enrolled Alex and began taking her on my way to work at 6:15 am. Laura, the pediatrician, frequently opened early for me and volunteered to take Alex home with her if I was caught at work. She understood as well as anyone that the surgery schedule was unpredictable. I blindly hit the jackpot of all daycares and took a big sigh of relief. I collected Alex each evening on my way back from the gym after work so Sandra was left with nothing to do. But she remained, sitting in her chair while I was away, secluding herself in her bedroom when I was home. After I fed Alex, I fixed my own dinner, ate, and put the dishes in the sink to be washed later, played in the yard, read, and sat for long periods with my daughter in our recliner in the living room before putting her to bed. After she was down, I finished my nightly chores and sat quietly in my chair, still attempting to get a handle on what had transpired in the last nine months and how I would move forward with Alex.

Only a month had passed, but I already missed having an adult around—an adult who wasn't Sandra. My cure was to work out even harder. I went about it with a fervor that was soon noticed by the gym owner. Soon, I was offered a regimen of supplements that had been recently taken off the market for being too much like anabolic steroids. I found myself spending $300 per month on pills to allow me to recover more quickly from my monstrous workouts. And just that easily, I fell back into my old addiction to more—absolutely intoxicated with something I could finally put my arms around and control. Something I hadn't been able to do in the previous nine months. Something I couldn't even do in my own home with my mother-in-law. When I came to my senses a few months later, screaming at my boss in the middle of our busy operating room hallway, I knew it was time to quit the supplements if not the obsessive exercising.

I'd accomplished an immense amount in a short amount of time—I was terribly busy with work, working out, caring for Alex, and keeping house. But I was still lonely. And I couldn't figure out how to meet people. Going to the mall and the local park on the weekends with Alex in tow garnered a lot of appreciative, even endearing looks, but no sudden offers for dinner or coffee. And I was at a loss as to how to initiate a conversation that would lead to a date. For that matter, dating seemed like it would be uncomfortable with the short amount of time that had elapsed since Joan's death, the fact that Sandra still lived with me, and mostly because of my story. I now carried a load of baggage. Of course, my family expressed concern that my timing was quite early, too, but I was on a mission to move on. I eventually allowed two friends from work to set me up, but both dates were failures through no fault of the lovely women who agreed to meet me.

Then I came up with the bright idea of asking out the physician who had cared for Joan throughout her transplant. Besides Joan's favorite nurse, Lori was the only adult with whom I'd connected on a deeply personal level throughout our stay in the hospital. She'd always inquired about Alex and even shopped for her on occasion. The fact that she was interested in my daughter and already knew my story further contributed to my conviction that we had potential. She was approximately my age and had absolutely endeared herself to me as an authentic and compassionate woman. She was also much like Joan, strong, self-confident, highly intelligent, and communicative.

Acquiring her phone number required the full force of my considerable will, but she did finally agree to meet me at a trendy restaurant—one I chose specifically to impress her with how hip I was.

I arrived fifteen minutes early and took a seat at the bar to await her arrival.

Feeling conspicuous, with people so close I could smell their boozy breath, I played unwilling participant in their intimate conversations. My once trendy clothes felt years out of date. Still overweight, I had deep, dark circles under my eyes from chronic lack of sleep, and my too-short hair, I'd noticed in the mirror as I prepared for my date, was beginning to thin. With nothing better to do while I waited, I ordered a drink for the first time since Joan's wake just to have something besides my extreme discomfort to focus on. After waiting for an hour, half of my warm gin and tonic still in its tumbler, I rose to leave, alone. Just then, Lori walked through the door. By the look on her face and the way she carried herself, I sensed our relationship was over before it had even begun.

32

"I Will Be Here"

The sky was the muted Midwest blue of August. A bald eagle circled lazily above, looking for an easy meal. Mosquitos buzzed occasionally by—the only sound over the constant roar of water flowing through the dam in the distance. Today, the flow was relatively low. In the spring, as Joan lay dying, it would have been a torrent. I watched small eddies, the water at the edge of the channel, come and go as they slipped into the bay off to the side, just past the walking trail and the fire pit of my campsite.

I was at a small campground below the dam on Red Rock Lake, on the Des Moines River, a place where I had always sought solace as a teenager. I'd scheduled a full week off from my no longer new job.

I'd come to mourn. To lay to rest my memories of my life with Joan. I'd come to feel God. I was far enough removed from Joan's death to know I must let her go before I could really live again. This was my church. Grass. Trees. Water. Sky. A safe place to let loose my grief. A quiet place to hear God.

But try as I might, my memories refused to come. I turned on my MP3 player—the play list I'd custom made for this very occasion. The songs I'd played for Joan, never my favorite, but hers. So familiar to my ears. They swept through my consciousness, evoking vestiges of emotion, but without the desired effect on my memory. Then the one I'd reserved as the piece de resistance, Steven Curtis Chapman's "I Will Be Here." This was one of two songs I'd sung to her at our wedding, slow dancing, melody coming softly from my lips pressed against her left ear, the song I played one thousand times in each of the hospital rooms she'd lain in on the small CD player that was ever present.

"In the morning when you wake up and the sun does not appear, I—I—I—I—I... I will be here..."

Still nothing.

"If in the darkness you lose sight of love, hold my hand and have no fear, I—I—I—I—I... I will be here."

It was just over seven weeks since Joan's death, five since I laid her to rest, four weeks and six days since I woke up alone in my bed—happy and comfortable with the sounds of the daughter I was enthralled by, buoyed by the distant hope that I might finally become the good man and father Joan always felt me to be, and yet slightly disappointed I hadn't gone through with my seduction of the barmaid. I was becoming desperate for the soft touch of a woman, any woman, so desperate that I was willing to allow the possibility of sleeping with a barmaid or a casual stranger. I already felt like I was slipping back from my new, "better" identity.

Grandpa and Grandma Dixon had agreed to watch Alex for the

week. Insisted, really. They were ravenous for her attention, as if they could still glean some essence of Joan from her touch.

I understood. Alex's touch was now my only physical comfort. Her soft, supple skin still evoked a warm tingle each time she reached out to me as her father. Each time her tiny, pudgy fingers grasped mine. Each time she gently touched my cheek or brushed my hair. Each time she smiled the smile so uniquely hers, with the smallest hint of her mother.

But I couldn't bring her here with me. Grieving was something I imagined I would do best alone. And yet, Alex was one of my few remaining cues to remember Joan. My memory of Joan's face was already clouded. I recalled her touch, her feel, her smell, but not her face. I wondered how little time must pass before I ceased to remember her at all, something in my darker moments I wished for. We'd been together seven years, and I already relied on her eight-by-ten "poster" portrait to spur visual memories.

Now nothing. Grief refused to come. Boredom came instead. Boredom was still trouble.

I flipped the switch on my phone. Reception was spotty, but enough to receive my messages. Jan, the Omaha City police woman I met once for coffee through a co-worker and had been talking with sporadically by phone ever since, had left a message. She had raven black hair and a confident swagger. She was drop dead gorgeous. Athletic. She was also involved, but her long-term boyfriend was contracting for Blackwater in Iraq. She was lonely like me.

Her message was short. "I have a weekend off. I was wondering if you wanted a visitor at the lake."

My plans for grieving thwarted and hopes of feeling closer to God dashed, I anticipated the hot, almost desperate scene as she showed up. I knew it wouldn't take long for us to stumble frantically into the queen-sized bed in the upper bedroom of my parent's camper.

I called her back and left a message. She never called back. She never came. I never saw her again. With a mix of disappointment and relief, I recognized that God may have been working on the small things in my life after all.

33

Happily Ever After

Thanksgiving night in Iowa with my family. Alex was passed around and around. Sufficiently doted upon by my entire family. She was engaging and irresistible, not just to me, but to all around her, just like her mother. I could already see Joan in her gestures, in the spacing of her eyes and their color of molten chocolate with those shocking little flecks of gold. She crawled from person to person, but always ended up in the pile of books, up one step, over the wooden parquet floor, and into the living room off which was my childhood bedroom-cum-playroom.

When my phone rang, I picked it from my pocket, taking note of the whispers at the periphery of the room. Someone asked surreptitiously, "Who's that?"

I didn't care if they knew. I didn't care if they disapproved. I knew what I was doing.

I'd finally reached out to the very woman Joan had once asked me to marry. Completely without romantic plans, though, love had never crossed my mind—much like sex before marriage never really crossed my mind with Joan. Loy lived 1,200 miles away in Montana. She seemed safe. A woman who knew and loved Joan. Unmarried. A safe repository for my loneliness and pain.

But after three months of email, we'd had our first phone conversation.

Joan's brother, Todd, once told me she could have been Joan's twin. I did not find that to be the case. Loy's voice had been crisp, clean, almost terse in contrast to Joan's, so soft and smooth. And Loy spoke matter-of-factly, distinctly—very little room for interpretation—the direct antithesis of Joan's, always searching for the gentlest way. Loy seemed completely opposite, in fact, something which intrigued me even more. Something different would surely guarantee an easier road.

By Thanksgiving, we had spoken every night since our first conversation by phone. I wouldn't have missed this evening's call for anything.

Months later, in the early summer, Loy came for a first visit. We walked around the lake that Joan and I had once strolled around, prior to her last admission. No trees to speak of, only rolling hills—rolling like Joan's contraction pattern on the day of Alex's birth—and a bike path surrounding the slightly murky, mud-and-algae-choked water. The sky was a washed-out blue—the vivid colors of spring had transitioned languidly into early summer. The humidity wasn't yet unbearable. I felt a sort of comfort as the not-yet-too-heavy air wrapped itself around us. Alex was in her stroller. I pushed. Loy walked along our left side, slightly ahead, until she abruptly stopped and said with a grin, "She keeps staring at me. It's making me kind of uncomfortable." Alex was indeed staring at her—staring right through her—as if attempting to determine who Loy was to us, how her mother Joan, who looked so different, smelled so different, who acted so differently, suddenly become this other person.

Loy and I married the next July in a public park, under a gazebo, in St. Helena, California. Pastor Wray officiated with only his wife, Ingrid, and our immediate family in attendance. Loy was beautiful in her lavender dress. Blue eyes sparkling, blond hair highlighted by the afternoon sun. The air was warm, but drier, as only the air in California wine country can be. The ceremony lasted only a few minutes. I held Alex the entire time. After all, she was as much a part of this union as Loy and me. We married after three dates—the first of which I didn't even know if I would recognize her when we finally met (again). She was beautiful, she was engaging, she was—I already knew—loyal. Alex had a mother. I had a partner. We sought to make a new start in Montana.

[34]

Cliff

Five years later, I sat in my car at the edge of a cliff, one foot on the accelerator, one on the brake. Long past the point of caring if the God who had failed Joan and me—the God who I only glimpsed in fleeting moments through Alex—would care that I was about to commit a mortal sin.

Moments before, I'd confronted Loy and told her I no longer wished to be married to her. I'd called her a selfish, harsh, uncaring woman. Her transgression: Not loving Alex. Her direct manner of communication which I'd found so refreshing when we first met, now seemed harsh and unloving as it pertained to the real love of my life—Alex. My decision to leave wasn't rash. Loy had just never become a part of Alex and my little family, as much as I yearned for a partner. Alex and I were inseparable, which left no room for another,

especially with Joan's ghost still felt strongly by me. I felt hopeless—
had for some time. I fled as Loy collapsed into a fetal position on
the bathroom floor, but her wails of despair followed me to my car.

I had only heard that sound once before. The sound of a mother
mourning the death of her child on a rutted dirt road in the middle
of a jungle a million miles from my home. Only the sun, a few scattered clouds, and hordes of insects bore witness to her keening.

Still, I'd sped recklessly away, down our gravel lane, finally coming to at the top of a cliff, nothing but sky, hills, and grass.

I couldn't drive my car off the cliff. Alex had become an integral
part of my being, and just like the first morning, in her lime green
rocker after Joan's funeral and the night flirting with the barmaid,
I sensed that God had placed this little gift in my life to help me
glimpse His love. When I breathed, she breathed. When I awoke, she
awoke. It had been this way since that morning in the rocking chair
watching the sun rise. I was unable to leave her.

When I returned home, Loy was still there. Alex was still at
school. Our dog was still splayed out awkwardly on the hardwood
floor next to the piano.

Loy and I weren't able to talk just then, but as time passed, we
sought counseling. We each softened and made tentative sorties into
the other's private thoughts. Our conversations started with little
things, then more important things, then to real discussions about
what we both wanted. I wanted to be happy. So did she. I wanted to
be loved. So did she. I wanted to be heard. So did she. I wanted her
to love Alex. She told me that without Alex, she would have already
gone. I believed her. Subconsciously, I had always believed she would
leave. After all, Joan had. Now a seed of trust that she would stay

was planted. Though my relationship with God was still tentative and sporadic, I can see now our new willingness to understand each other must have been a gift from Him. Loy and I had been too far gone to have ever come to terms on our own.

Making room in my life for Loy had unexpected consequences. I also made room in Alex's life for her. Though Alex and I had both believed we had a perfect father daughter relationship, I was forced to consider that I had been somehow keeping her and Loy from forming their own bond, and that I had been using her as an unwitting emotional crutch. I stopped forcing Alex to remain only a part of me and allowed her to be her own person. When she became an entity unto herself, her life changed, too, and her relationship with Loy flourished. Loy was able to show her the love she had always felt. And I was able to recognize that love, different as it was from my particular brand. And through this revelation that mine wasn't the only type of love, I understood at least for a moment that maybe God had been loving me all along.

[35]

Water

Six months later, I hiked alone into the Bob Marshall Wilderness, a magical mystical place. My base camp was to be Holland Lake Lodge. This was the spot where Joan had spent her week with Loy and Christian prior to her diagnosis, just prior to becoming pregnant. Joan would have been in her khaki shorts and a t-shirt with ankle socks and hikers. Her hair in a pony set just above the strap of her tennis visor. Loy in convertible pants, sturdier shoes, and a hiking cap with her fleece tied around her waist.

I held a clear image of Joan and Loy sitting slightly hunched on a log at the top of Holland Falls, breath coming in short gasps from exertion, the beauty of the thousand-mile view, and the overwhelming power of the waterfall right next to them. The spring runoff roaring over the cliff and through the canyon. Spray saturating everything within a hundred feet. The lone log beneath their perch vibrating, almost humming, with the energy of the water crashing against and over it. They wouldn't have talked in this place. It was beyond words.

I had already visited this spot two years after Joan's death with Loy, Alex, and my parents, but I was so preoccupied with my new marriage and distracted by my undealt with grief that I couldn't yet feel the significance of the place. Alex, clad only in saggy, water-logged diapers, had waded fearlessly into the cold, clear water. Loy, jeans rolled to her knees, at her side, holding her tiny hand. The sky was a smoky gray, the water reflected a shimmering upside-down picture of the peaks above, only one still capped with snow. A fire had been burning for a week just over the ridge beyond the lake. We were on alert to evacuate, but the call hadn't yet been made. As darkness fell, the fire which was just out of sight cast an eerie orange glow, outlining the ridge with molten lava, but now it was midday, and we were enjoying the last of summer. Suddenly a gigantic helicopter swooped down, roaring—thirstily slurping massive amounts of lake water into its belly. I gave a sudden start, remembering helicopter rides in a different life time. Momentarily caught just on the edge of alarm. The helicopter sank slowly lower, rotors disrupting the glassy surface with the beautiful transposed painting of the lake with its towering mountains above. Rotor wash kicked up pine needles from shore and turned them into miniature missiles. Alex stopped suddenly—mid play. She couldn't have known my panic. The pilot turned the nose of his machine directly toward her. Horror playing through my mind. Gunship, rotating toward her. Minnie guns coming to bear. He waved—a casual, cocky half-salute. Alex screamed with glee and threw both hands to the sky as if she could reach out and touch this enormous thing, a fitting end to our visit that was rightfully more about Alex than about God and me.

———

This time, I was alone. I'd come to hear the voice of God. The thunderous Charlton Heston-like voice. I wanted Him to tell me He loved me. I wanted Him to tell me I was alright. I wanted Him to pat me on the back and say, "Well done. You've finally become the man I knew you could be."

I set up camp along the shore and spent three days completely alone kayaking and fishing, all the while listening intently, but hearing nothing. A sense of familiarity as I remembered my failed attempt at mourning by Lake Red Rock in my parent's camper. Having set up the perfect opportunity for God to speak to me and hearing nothing but the clanging of a country western band at a wedding reception at the lodge for three days, I grew frustrated.

Wanting to dive deeper into my "church of the wilderness," I planned to hike miles into Bob Marshall Wilderness to a serene, high mountain lake; to spend a couple of nights listening to the great nothing, hoping finally to hear the voice of my God. My journey began with three liters of water, a filter, and only a few granola bars to sustain me. I planned on using my lack of food, the direct antithesis to my previous need for more, to adjust my mind and tune into my heavenly conversation. I'd begun fasting over a week prior to prepare my mind and spirit for this. I'd adopted the "Daniel Fast," with only fruits and vegetables—a fast the Adventists seemed gung ho about. I'd made my peace with the Adventists, joining the church Loy had always been a member of. Pausing by the log that I imagined Joan and Loy sitting on as they looked out on the vast valley and mountains beyond, I was cooled by the spray they once felt and heard the roar of the falls that drowned out all possibility of their conversation, and I felt too overwhelmed to get a fix on my feelings in this place, where the three of our lives intersected.

A mile later, ever upward, I experienced the first hints of cramps in my thighs, but I pressed on. By the time I reached Upper Holland Lake, I was halfway through my water. I lunched on a boulder the size of a large building. This lake was smaller, even more serene, no other person on or near it. A slight breeze wafted around me. Small trout surfaced, ripples rolling slowly toward every shore. The sky was crystal blue, unlike the hazy, smoky day with Alex in the lake. Reflections of cream puff clouds over the neighboring peaks lent a drowsy sense of peace to my respite. I rested against my pack in my sweat soaked clothes and took in the vastness of the great Bob Marshall. I knew I hadn't brought enough food, but instead of reversing my trail, I chose to continue upward along the entire seventeen-mile loop.

I continued my hike with purpose, noting vaguely that the temperature was now nearly ninety degrees by my pocket thermometer. My path took me ever upward, and I tricked myself as I neared every bend in the path into thinking that around the next corner, past the next switchback, I would find a path through the mountains. I was soon in serious physical danger. With so little to drink that the sheer act of digestion would require too much water, I forwent any of the scanty food I'd packed. I was cramping badly. The ambient temperature hovered between eighty and ninety degrees, and I was sweating profusely. The weather had been cold as I set out, and now I was overdressed. I passed two small lakes on my route, but in my haste and altered mental state, I neglected to use my filter at either of them. I even had iodine tablets and a small gas stove to boil the water if needed, but the fact that "salvation" was riding in my backpack didn't even cross my mind. After climbing another fifteen hundred feet and hiking several more miles, I sat to rest at the corner of yet another switchback and prayed. At that point, I had been forced to stop to rest every fifty to one hundred feet. As I rested, I told God I was unable to continue my trek over what looked like a pass still far in the distance. I told Him that if He wanted me to finish my hike home, He would have to be my energy.

Frustrated at hearing no voice, I arose for the last time and walked on. As I rounded the next corner, I spied an archway through the mountain, a passage beneath the peak that would allow me to begin my descent. I stood under the arch feeling relieved, but not at all spiritual, and I drank the last of my water. The five-mile descent, which was much longer than I'd expected, was torture on my cramping thighs and battered feet. The temperature remained in the low nineties, and I soon regretted having finished the last of my water. Another three and a half miles of difficult walking, and I was at the point of giving up again—relegated to shuffling down the mountain, almost to the point of crawling. But as I was about to sit and attempt once more to call upon God, two hikers appeared. The first thing they said was, "Are you out of water?"

Freedom

Another year passed, and I had one final piece to my puzzle—the one I was unable to accomplish at Lake Red Rock in my parents' camper. Loy returned with me to the banks of Holland Lake as I prepared to let go of the memory of Joan. We sat by the shore with Christian. For Christian seemed part of this too—owner, friend, fellow traveler, griever. I sensed within him a shared spirituality, with his steady gaze and sense of serenity. Together, we felt Holland Lake was hallowed ground. Though I'd heard no booming voice of God here, I'd sensed him nonetheless. He'd spoken to me through the strangers on the trail. I'd finally realized that God has always placed people on my trail, right before the road forks, to save me from myself. Beginning with my parents, old Lawrence Kingery in my adolescence, Joan as I desperately fought to become a man my parents would be proud of, Pastor Wray in the depths of my despair and questioning, Alex as I struggled to become a father, Loy as I wrestled with all of my old demons, and now Christian himself with his name that I felt was not at all a coincidence, who had welcomed us to his lodge.

The sun was already below the crests of the mountains—the same mountains that were once aglow with firelight. The moon was to our backs just above the pine forest. The lake again a placid mirror. The pebble floor ten feet below still hazily visible beneath its reflections. I sensed more than heard the distant roar of Holland Falls with its soaring view of the valley and mountains beyond. My heart beat faster—familiar in its pace, bringing me slowly back to that year of my life. Each beat brought Joan's visage more clearly into focus. Loy and Christian were there, but not there—witnesses, not participants.

The fire crackled and started, warmth stopped short by the memory of her. I was finally back there. Amid the astringent smell and harsh lights of her hospital room. High pitched beeps and screeches constant—no longer could I hear the roar of the falls. Back to the impossible decisions we had to make. Back to the hopelessness and shame of watching her die and my inability to save her. Back to my failure, at the time, to interpret what role, if any, God played in our story.

I had never given myself over completely to grief in the company of anyone. I silently wept. Tears rolled down my cheeks, falling, joining forever the clear waters of Holland Lake.

At the appointed time, Christian produced the wine bottle and glasses. V. Sattui Rutherford Vineyard Cabernet 1992. Joan's favorite. Complicated, intricate, full of character, just like her. I distantly recognized the muted pop of the cork as he pulled it from the bottle. The slosh of nectar on crystal as he poured.

The goblet was in my hand—smoky taste of the wine, first bite of its tannic acid gone as it slowly rolled past the tip of my tongue on its way toward my throat. Awash in memories. The year 2000. In the underground cellar of her favorite winery. Formal attire. Black tie for me with the Hugo Boss tux I'd purchased less than a year before. Joan in her stunning royal blue formal gown, glowing, cheeks with a hint of blush that gave away her excitement. Magical. The moment stretched and stretched.

Finally, Loy handed me my paper. I didn't need it. I'd memorized the words. "Tonight, in the presence of two people I love, two people you have loved, I release you. I will always love you. Tonight, I set your memory free. Tonight, I am free."

Freedom. What did that mean? I was finally free to love another fully. I was finally free to love myself. I was finally free to love God in a less needy way. But I was also free to slip into my old ways. I was free to harm others. Sometimes I feared I would. I feared I would never do another selfless, kind, or loving thing for any other person again. I would again become a slave to my own selfish tendencies.

Maybe my life would have been simpler if I'd remained a single man. Certainly, it might have been lived with less pain. But I'd chosen a different path. Though I'd fought and fought, failed, and tried again, once I'd finally pledged my undying love for Joan in the garden in Orlando, I'd become a better person. I'd tied myself to another and vowed I would never leave or forsake her. That is what God had promised me—promised us all—that he wouldn't leave nor forsake us. And though I was free to choose and far from godly, when I said in the hospital room I was "all in," I meant it—leaving was no longer a possibility. Though I hadn't necessarily felt ready, once I'd met my one and only daughter, I fell so deeply in love, it was impossible not to consider her in every decision I made henceforth. When I finally committed to Loy, not by saying the words at our wedding, but by arriving with her at this moment on Holland Lake, I gave myself to her with my whole being and became the husband I had always wanted to be, the husband God wanted me to be. I was free, but not in ways I had once expected. I set the paper on fire and released it to the wind, remembering the day I loosed Joan's ashes on the highest hilltop of her family's homestead overlooking the meandering Niaobrara River in Nebraska. Her remains had exploded violently, as if they'd been chafing for this release from the box that had bound them, into the blustery swirling wind on the hilltop. How they circled back toward me, and I watched helplessly, unable to move as grey specks and small pieces of bone landed on and clung to my blue knit sweater.

This evening, the ashes of the paper moved silently into the darkness, floating gracefully on a swirling updraft above the lake, before slowly, elegantly settling into the crisp, clear water. Finally, with clarity, I knew I was free. I was free to become a good man only by giving myself fully to others, by loving them fully. Only then, I began to understand love… and to feel loved by my God.

Made in the USA
Lexington, KY
26 March 2018